# Connected Packaging: The Game-Changing Marketing Tool

## About the Author

Jenny Stanley is a highly accomplished business owner and visionary leader with over 20 years of global experience in sales and business management within the B2B Media and Creative Technology industry. As the sole owner and Managing Director of Appetite Creative, founded in 2015, Jenny has positioned the company among the global leaders in Connected Packaging.

Under her leadership, Appetite Creative has become one of the world's few creative technology companies with a specialised focus in this innovative sector. The company bridges the gap between brands and their audiences in the digital age by leveraging technology, creativity, and strategic thinking to create immersive and interactive experiences that resonate deeply with consumers. Notable clients include - Coca-Cola, Tetra Pak, Pepsi Co, Greiner Packaging, SIG, Elopack and Bacardi.

In addition to their creative services, Appetite Creative offers comprehensive consulting services in the field of Connected Packaging. Jenny herself serves as a consultant, sharing her expertise to help brands navigate this rapidly evolving landscape. This dual approach of creative execution and strategic consulting allows Appetite Creative to provide end-to-end solutions for clients looking to leverage Connected Packaging in their marketing strategies.

Jenny's expertise is demonstrated through her strategic operations, business growth optimization, and the launch of the first Global Connected Packaging Survey, which provides valuable insights from marketing professionals worldwide. Appetite Creative also runs a webinar series and a podcast called "The Talking Giraffe," featuring notable guests from companies like Nestle, Kellogg's, Tetra Pak, SIG, Amazon, and AIPIA. Furthermore, they host the annual Global Connected Packaging Summit, the first virtual summit dedicated to Connected Packaging.

Jenny's dedication to fostering connectivity across industries led her to establish FemmeNiche, a dynamic women's networking group aimed at inspiring and supporting women from diverse backgrounds and industries. Her leadership and strategic vision have solidified Appetite Creative as a global leader in Connected Packaging.

Appetite Creative operates with core values that include a commitment to diversity, inclusivity, eco-friendly practices, and sustainable packaging solutions. The company's team is composed of talented individuals from diverse cultural and ethnic backgrounds, fuelling their innovative approach. They encourage a culture of ongoing learning and professional development to stay ahead in the ever-evolving digital landscape.

With a diverse portfolio spanning technology, packaging, food, e-commerce, automotive, and creative agencies, Appetite Creative delivers tailored services to meet each client's unique needs. Their achievements are reflected in numerous recognitions and industry awards, showcasing their dedication, creativity, and excellence in connected packaging solutions.

Jenny holds a Bachelor's Degree in Business Management and Marketing from Brunel University London. Originally from the UK, she moved to

Madrid, Spain, in 2014, where she quickly established her agency. Married with one daughter, Jenny is an avid horse lover who spends her free time in the equestrian world when she's not immersed in the digital realm.

She dedicates this book to her husband Pedro and her daughter Freya, with a note to follow your dreams and never forget: Lady Luck favours the brave!

# Contents

- **Near-Field Communication (NFC)**
- **QR V NFC**
- **Bluetooth Beacons and RFID**
- **Augmented Reality (AR)**
- **Digital Watermarking**

  **-Digimark**

  **-Polytag**

# Chapter 3: The Business Case for Connected Packaging

- **Marketing and Consumer Engagement**
  - **Enhancing customer experience and brand loyalty**
  - **Inclusivity and accessibility**

    **-Navilens**

- **Supply Chain Management**
  - **Improving traceability and inventory control**
  - **Authentication**
  - **- Scantrust and laava**
- **Sustainability and Regulatory Compliance**
  - **Meeting environmental standards and regulations**

# Chapter 4: Case Studies and Industry Examples

- **Leading Brands and Success Stories**
  - **In-depth analysis of successful campaigns**

**Emmi, KDD, Don Simon, Gulf Union, Jus de caribes, Gooday, Tetra Pak sustainability**

- **Lessons Learned**

- Insights from both successes and challenges faced

## Chapter 5: The Consumer Experience

- **Interactive Engagement**
  - **How consumers interact with Connected Packaging**
- **Behavioural Insights**
  - **Understanding consumer behaviour and preferences**
- **Feedback and Analytics**
  - **Leveraging data to improve engagement**

## Chapter 6: Designing and Implementing Connected Packaging

- **Strategic Planning**
  - **Identifying goals and objectives**
- **Design Considerations**
  - **Balancing aesthetics and functionality**
- **Implementation Strategies**
  - **Steps to integrate Connected Packaging into existing processes**

## Chapter 7: Future Trends in Connected Packaging

- **Emerging Technologies**
  - **AI, IoT, and other innovations on the horizon**
- **Market Predictions**
  - **Forecasts and future directions for the industry**
- **Potential Challenges**
  - **Addressing potential obstacles and limitations**

# Chapter 8: Regulatory and Ethical Considerations

- **Compliance and Standards**
  - **Key regulations and industry standards**
- **Privacy and Security**
  - **Ensuring consumer data protection**
- **Ethical Marketing Practices**
  - **Balancing marketing goals with consumer trust**

# Chapter 9: Conclusions

- **The Impact of Connected Packaging**
  - **Recap of key points and future outlook**
- **Summary of thoughts and recommendations**
- **Final Word**
- **Glossary of Terms**
  - **Definitions of key terms and acronyms**
  - **Resources and further reading**

## Introduction

Connected Packaging leverages advanced technologies like QR codes, NFC tags, RFID, Bluetooth beacons, and augmented reality (AR) to create dynamic consumer interactions. Imagine scanning a QR code on a cereal box to receive a personalised breakfast recipe or tapping an NFC chip on a beverage bottle to join a brand's loyalty program instantly. These experiences not only enhance consumer engagement but also provide brands with critical insights into consumer behaviour and preferences.

The rise of Connected Packaging can be traced back to early innovations such as barcodes and QR codes, which laid the groundwork for today's more sophisticated solutions. As technology advanced, so did the capabilities of packaging, evolving from simple identifiers to complex communication tools. This evolution reflects the broader digital transformation occurring across industries, where connectivity and data are central to business success.

As a digital experiences studio specialising in connected packaging, Appetite Creative has been at the forefront of this revolution. The team has witnessed firsthand the transformative power of turning product packaging into a media channel, helping brands across EMEA, Americas, and MENA regions to create innovative, engaging experiences that bridge the physical and digital worlds.

Drawing on our extensive experience working with global brands like Bacardi, Pepsi, Starbucks, and Coca-Cola, this book aims to provide a comprehensive guide to the world of connected packaging. We'll share insights gained from real-world implementations, discuss best practices, and explore the future potential of this technology. Alongside short snippets and interviews with other leaders in this space from brand, manufacturing, printing, technology and industry body perspectives, this book aims to provide a comprehensive guide to the world of connected packaging. With our global presence, we'll provide a broad perspective on connected packaging trends and implementations across different markets and cultures.


**Overview of the Book and Its Objectives**

"Connected Packaging: The Game-Changing Marketing Tool" aims to provide a comprehensive guide to understanding and implementing Connected Packaging.

This book is designed to be a valuable resource for marketing professionals, packaging designers, brand managers, and anyone interested in the intersection of technology and consumer engagement. Whether you're new to the concept of connected packaging or looking to enhance your existing strategies, you'll find practical advice, inspiring examples, and forward-looking insights to help you harness the power of this transformative technology.

Throughout the chapters, I will share insights gained from real-world implementations, discuss best practices, and explore the future potential of this technology.

Exploring the history, technology, business case, design considerations, case studies, consumer experience, future trends, and regulatory aspects of Connected Packaging. Each chapter is structured to provide both theoretical insights and practical applications, ensuring readers can translate knowledge into actionable strategies.

The objectives of this book are:

**Educate Readers**: Provide a thorough understanding of what Connected Packaging is, how it works, and why it is important.

**Showcase Benefits:** Highlight the myriad benefits Connected Packaging offers to both businesses and consumers.

**Provide Practical Guidance**: Offer step-by-step strategies for designing and implementing Connected Packaging solutions.

**Share Real-World Examples:** Present case studies and industry examples to illustrate successful applications and lessons learned.

**Explore Future Trends:** Discuss emerging technologies and market predictions to prepare readers for the future of Connected Packaging.

**Address Regulatory and Ethical Considerations**: Ensure readers are aware of compliance requirements and best practices for ethical marketing.

By the end of this book, readers will have a clear understanding of the transformative potential of Connected Packaging and the tools needed to harness its power effectively.

## Definition and Importance of Connected Packaging

### Definition of Connected Packaging

Connected Packaging refers to the integration of digital technologies with traditional packaging to create an interactive and communicative system. Through technologies such as QR codes, NFC chips, RFID tags, Bluetooth beacons, and augmented reality, Connected Packaging allows consumers to interact with products using their smartphones or other connected devices. This interaction can provide a wealth of information, personalised experiences, and real-time data exchange between consumers and manufacturers.

### Importance of Connected Packaging

Connected Packaging is becoming increasingly important in today's market for several reasons:

**Enhanced Consumer Engagement:** Connected Packaging transforms passive packaging into an interactive experience. Consumers can access detailed product information, receive personalised offers, participate in loyalty programs, and engage with interactive content, all of which enhance their overall experience and satisfaction.

**Improved Product Transparency:** With Connected Packaging, consumers can easily verify product authenticity, check ingredient lists, view expiration dates, and access other essential details. This transparency fosters trust and helps consumers make informed purchasing decisions.

**Inclusivity**: Connected Packaging enhances inclusivity and accessibility by providing QR codes that translate product details, instructions, and ingredients into audio, aiding individuals with vision impairments and learning disabilities to shop and use items independently.

**Real-Time Tracking and Monitoring:** For manufacturers, Connected Packaging offers the ability to track products throughout the supply chain. This improves inventory management, prevents theft, ensures product quality, and provides valuable data for optimising logistics.

**Data-Driven Insights:** Connected Packaging enables the collection of valuable data on consumer behaviour, preferences, and usage patterns. This data can inform marketing strategies, product improvements, and overall business decisions.

**Targeted Marketing and Promotions:** Brands can use Connected Packaging to deliver personalised marketing campaigns. By leveraging data collected through consumer interactions, companies can offer tailored promotions, discounts, and loyalty programs that resonate with individual consumers.

**Sustainability and Responsible Consumption:** Connected Packaging can promote sustainability by providing recycling instructions, encouraging responsible consumption, and reducing waste through better inventory management. It also supports transparency in sourcing and production practices.

**Anti-Counterfeiting Measures:** By integrating security features such as unique identifiers, Connected Packaging helps verify product authenticity and protect against counterfeit goods. This ensures that consumers receive genuine products and helps maintain brand integrity.

**Strengthened Brand-Consumer Relationships:** Through personalised experiences and direct interactions, Connected Packaging helps build stronger connections between brands and consumers. This fosters loyalty and advocacy, driving repeat purchases and positive word-of-mouth.

Connected Packaging represents a significant shift in how brands interact with consumers and manage their products. It offers a myriad of benefits that extend beyond traditional packaging, making it a crucial component of modern marketing and supply chain strategies. As the digital landscape continues to evolve, Connected Packaging will play an essential role in shaping the future of consumer products and brand interactions, creating a more connected, transparent, and engaging marketplace.

In the following chapters, we will delve deeper into each of these aspects, exploring the history, technology, applications, and future trends of Connected Packaging. By the end of this book, you will have a comprehensive understanding of how to leverage Connected Packaging to stay ahead in the competitive landscape and meet the evolving needs of today's consumers.

# Chapter 1- The Evolution of Connected Packaging: A Chronological Journey

**A Chronological Journey**

### Historical Background

The roots of Connected Packaging can be traced back to the 1950s with the invention of barcodes, which laid the groundwork for product tracking and identification. Fifty years ago, on June 26, 1974, the first universal product code (UPC) was scanned at a Marsh Supermarket in Troy, Ohio on Wrigley's Juicy Fruit,, kicking off a retail and supply chain automation revolution. In the 1990s, the commercial introduction of barcodes and in 1994 QR (Quick Response) codes, marked a significant milestone, bridging physical products to digital information. QR Codes were first invented by a Japanese company, Denso Wave in 1994. An employee named Masahiro Hara conjured up the idea of QR codes while playing the game Go (it consists of a 19×19 grid with black and white stones placed throughout) and from there its inception firstly largely impacted South East Asia. The early 2000's saw the growth of the internet and mobile devices, prompting companies to explore ways to connect packaging to online content, such as printing QR codes that linked to websites and globally there was a shift towards the use of QR codes. QR codes have revolutionised how we interact with the world, from scanning a code to accessing a website to making payments.

## Early Innovations

One of the earliest documented examples of Connected Packaging was the "SmartLabel" case study from Jones Packaging in 2008. Their QR code labels enabled linking product packaging to online content of nutritional information and recipes, demonstrating an early use of QR codes to connect physical products to digital experiences.

The concept gained further momentum in 2009 with the coining of the term "Internet of Things" (IoT), envisioning a network of physical objects embedded with sensors, software, and connectivity. This paved the way for connected products and packaging. In the 2010's, the rise of NFC (Near-Field Communication) technology allowed smartphones to read embedded chips, enabling more advanced Connected Packaging applications beyond just QR codes. Major brands like Diageo, Macy's, and Kellogg's piloted Connected Packaging initiatives using NFC, QR codes, and Bluetooth beacons between 2015 and 2016.

Diageo's partnership with Thin Film to incorporate NFC tags in their Johnnie Walker Blue Label bottles in 2015 was a high-profile example, allowing customers to access brand content, verify authenticity, and even reorder products via NFC. Similarly, Kellogg's launched a "Connected JoyBowl " cereal box in 2016 that integrated on-pack graphics into a video game app through image recognition.

A significant milestone was reached in 2017 when Apple's iOS 11 introduced built-in QR code scanning in the Camera app, followed by Android 9 Pie in 2018, which added native QR scanning to the Google Camera app. This eliminated the need for third-party apps, making it seamless for users to access digital experiences connected to physical packaging via QR codes.

In 2018, Appetite Creative, my global brand experience agency, launched our first Connected Packaging campaign with Shazam and CurryKing, a German brand, featuring a series of games where winners could win a microwave. It was so successful that the brand decided to keep running for another 3 months making it a 6 month campaign.

The COVID-19 pandemic in 2019/ 2020 further accelerated the adoption of QR codes in daily life, from vaccination certificates to contactless menus in restaurants, underscoring the importance of Connected Packaging solutions. Insider Intelligence eMarketer reported that the US market alone saw an impressive 25% growth in smartphone users scanning a QR code in 2020, nearly doubling the 12.6% increase in 2019.

2021- The use of QR codes is on the rise with the Marketing Charts 2021 report revealing that 54 percent of young adults aged 18-29 are the most likely to scan marketing QR codes in the US alone. Their report also revealed the following: 48% of 30–44-year-old consumers scanned marketing QR codes and 44% of those aged 45–64 scanned marketing QR codes.

2022- Coca Cola and ABinBev declare QR codes are now part of their always on strategy and will feature on all their products. The marketing applications of QR codes start to grow rapidly in the food and beverage sector.

2023- Pepsi reveals using QR codes during 2022 in the US enabled them to increase their CRM database by 50%. Statista releases data that 44.6% of internet users had scanned a QR code at least once.

2024- The Connected Packaging Report by Appetite Creative reveals that 88% of brands surveyed plan to use a QR code in 2024.

**Technological Advancements**

Technological advancements like digital watermarking (e.g., Digimarc Barcode, Iconspire), blockchain integration for supply chain transparency, and the integration of Connected Packaging with voice assistants and augmented reality (AR) experiences continued to shape the landscape.

The evolution of Connected Packaging has been significantly driven by technological advancements. Key innovations like Near-Field Communication (NFC), Bluetooth beacons, and digital watermarking have transformed the landscape of how physical products connect with digital content.

**Near-Field Communication (NFC)**

Near-Field Communication (NFC) technology emerged as a pivotal innovation in Connected Packaging during the 2010's. This technology enables smartphones and other devices to establish communication with NFC-enabled tags embedded in product packaging, offering a range of functionalities:

**Authentication:** Consumers can verify the authenticity of a product, helping to combat counterfeiting.

**Engagement:** Brands can offer interactive content, such as videos, promotions, and detailed product information, enhancing the consumer experience.

**Reordering:** Customers can reorder products by simply tapping their smartphone on the NFC tag, streamlining the purchasing process.

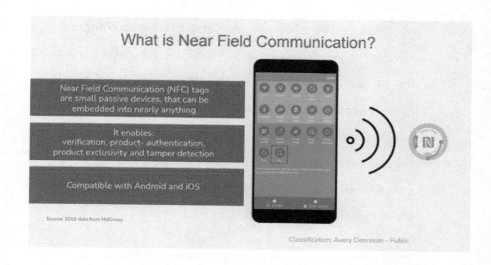

A notable early example of NFC in Connected Packaging was Diageo's partnership with Thin Film in 2015. They incorporated NFC tags into Johnnie Walker Blue Label bottles, allowing customers to access brand content, verify authenticity, and reorder products seamlessly.

**Industry Adoption and Perception**

According to Blue Bite's data **Connected product interactions have increased 723% since 2018**. On the whole, Blue Bite's industry data revealed that connected technology usage rose over 1,000% between 2018 and 2022.

More and more brands and consumers are using NFC and QR technology as they see its potential.

As of 2022, the NFC market was valued at $23.1 billion, according to a report from Emergen Research. At a compound annual growth rate of 14.2%, the NFC market is predicted to be worth $87.53 billion by 2032. More than a third of respondents in a survey from S&P Global indicated they were using their contactless cards more often because of tap-to-pay technology. The data makes it clear that consumers are increasingly familiar with and using NFC, which makes it easy for brands to adopt the technology and enable their products.

These statistics highlight the growing importance of NFC in the connected packaging landscape, with brands recognising the potential to deliver premium experiences and engage consumers effectively.

**Bluetooth Beacons**

Bluetooth beacons, a revolutionary technology, have significantly enhanced the potential of the IoT world and Connected Packaging. These small, cost-effective devices emit signals detectable by nearby smartphones, enabling a myriad of location-based interactions. Key applications of Bluetooth beacons include **proximity marketing,** where retailers send personalised offers and promotions to consumers' smartphones when they are near specific products or displays. Additionally, beacons facilitate in-store navigation by guiding customers through the store, thus enhancing their shopping experience with precise directions to desired products.

Furthermore, businesses can leverage beacons for **data collection**, gathering insights on consumer behaviour and movement patterns within a store, which can inform strategic marketing and optimise store layouts.

The advent of iBeacon technology, introduced by Apple in 2013, has been a game-changer in the retail industry. iBeacon utilises Bluetooth Low Energy (BLE) to transmit signals from beacons to smartphones, enabling the delivery of hyper-contextual content based on the user's location. This technology has bridged the gap between online and offline retail, allowing retailers to engage proactively with customers both inside and around the store premises. iBeacon's capability to send promotional messages and alerts to potential customers in various locations, such as malls, restaurants, and museums, has transformed the retail landscape, driving increased sales and enhancing customer experiences.

- **Proximity Marketing**: Retailers can send personalised offers and promotions to consumers' smartphones when they are near a specific product or display.

- **In-Store Navigation:** Beacons can guide customers through a store, enhancing their shopping experience by providing directions to specific products.

- **Data Collection**: Businesses can gather data on consumer behaviour and movement patterns within a store, informing marketing strategies and store layouts.

Several real-world instances highlight the effective application of iBeacon technology in retail. Macy's, an American department store chain, was one of the early adopters, using BLE beacons to personalise and enhance the shopping experience. By integrating beacons with the Shopkick app, Macy's provided real-time information and notifications about discounts and promotions based on customers' in-store interactions and online browsing histories. Similarly, British luxury clothing retailer Ted Baker utilised iBeacon technology in its Westfield White City shop in London. Beacons installed in mannequins detected nearby customers' smartphones, triggering push notifications with detailed product descriptions, photos, and additional offers, thus enhancing customer engagement and satisfaction.

The benefits of iBeacon technology for the retail industry are manifold. BLE beacons can significantly improve customer engagement and satisfaction by offering personalised discounts, loyalty programs, and enhanced in-store experiences. Retailers can gather valuable data on customer preferences and behaviour, enabling the creation of targeted marketing strategies and personalised offers. Furthermore, beacons facilitate retargeting efforts, allowing retailers to re-engage customers who left the store without making a purchase by sending tailored offers and promotions. The affordability of beacon technology, coupled with its low power consumption and compatibility with both Android and iOS platforms, makes it a cost-effective solution for enhancing customer engagement and driving sales.

In conclusion, Bluetooth beacons and iBeacon technology have the potential to revolutionise the retail industry by modernising customer interactions in brick-and-mortar stores. More about the retail experience rather than the packaging itself. Retailers who embrace this technology can expect increased brand visibility, enhanced customer engagement, and improved sales performance. With the rise of smartphone usage and mobile shopping trends, beacons serve as a critical link between the digital and physical retail spaces, ensuring that businesses stay competitive in an ever-evolving market.

**Digital Watermarking**

Digital watermarking, including technologies like Digimarc Barcode, Iconspire and more recently Polytag, has further advanced the Connected Packaging field. These watermarks are invisible to the naked eye but can be detected by smartphones and other devices, enabling a variety of applications:

- **Enhanced Product Information:** Consumers can scan the packaging to access detailed product information, including ingredients, usage instructions, and promotional content.

- **Supply Chain Transparency**: Watermarks can track products throughout the supply chain, enhancing traceability and ensuring product safety and authenticity.

- **Interactive Experiences**: Brands can create interactive experiences, such as augmented reality (AR) features that engage consumers and provide a deeper connection to the product.

The drawback currently here is that digital watermarking needs an app or special technology to recognise the watermark at this time. QR codes and NFC technology is now already installed into all smartphones without the need to download anything else.

We look deeper into Digital watermarking in the next chapter.

**Blockchain Integration**

Blockchain technology has been integrated into Connected Packaging to enhance supply chain transparency and security. By recording each transaction in a secure and immutable ledger, blockchain ensures that product information is accurate and tamper-proof. This technology supports:

- **Traceability:** Consumers and stakeholders can track the journey of a product from its origin to the point of sale, ensuring transparency and authenticity.

- **Anti-Counterfeiting**: Blockchain helps in verifying the authenticity of products, protecting both brands and consumers from counterfeit goods.

- **Sustainability**: Companies can use blockchain to document the environmental impact of their products, providing consumers with information about sustainable practices and encouraging responsible consumption.

## Augmented Reality (AR) Experiences

AR technology has brought a new dimension to Connected Packaging by overlaying digital information onto the physical world. AR applications in packaging include:

- **Interactive Content**: Consumers can use their smartphones to view animations, videos, and 3D models that appear on the packaging, enhancing the unboxing experience.

- **Educational Tools:** Brands can offer educational content through AR, such as step-by-step instructions, tutorials, and product demonstrations.

- **Gaming**: AR can turn packaging into an interactive game, creating a fun and engaging experience for consumers, especially in the case of products targeted at younger audiences.

In summary, technological advancements such as NFC, Bluetooth beacons, digital watermarking, blockchain integration, and AR have revolutionised Connected Packaging. These innovations have enhanced consumer engagement, improved supply chain transparency, and provided new opportunities for brands to interact with their customers in meaningful ways. As technology continues to evolve, the potential for Connected Packaging will only expand, offering even more sophisticated and immersive experiences.

These innovations have enhanced consumer engagement, improved supply chain transparency, and provided new opportunities for brands to interact with their customers in meaningful ways. As technology continues to evolve, the potential for Connected Packaging will only expand, offering even more sophisticated and immersive experiences.

## Legislation Changes and Impact on Connected Packaging

### Digital Product Passport (DPP) and Regulatory Advances

The introduction of the Digital Product Passport (DPP) in March 2024 by the European Union, as part of the proposed Ecodesign for Sustainable Products Regulation (ESPR), marks a significant advancement in regulatory efforts. The DPP aims to enhance transparency and provide comprehensive information about a product's value chain, including origin, materials, environmental impact, and disposal recommendations. This initiative aligns with the growing demand for transparency from consumers and stakeholders, facilitating informed decision-making and promoting sustainability.

### Extended Producer Responsibility (EPR)

Complementing the DPP, Extended Producer Responsibility (EPR) has emerged as a pivotal strategy in sustainable development. EPR shifts the responsibility for post-consumer waste management from municipalities and consumers back to producers, encouraging sustainable product design and resource efficiency. This policy approach compels producers to internalise the environmental costs of their products, leading to more sustainable designs that are easier to recycle, repair, and reuse.

**Economic and Environmental Incentives**

EPR policies often include economic incentives such as tax breaks and subsidies for sustainable practices, alongside penalties for non-compliance. These financial mechanisms motivate companies to adopt environmentally friendly practices. For example, the Tire Stewardship BC program in British Columbia includes an Advance Disposal Fee on new tires, which funds the recycling and management of scrap tires.

**Technological Integration**

Digital capabilities play a crucial role in EPR compliance and optimization. Advanced data management and analytics allow manufacturers to track and report environmental impacts, ensuring adherence to EPR regulations. Tools like the Digital Product Passport and IoT enhance supply chain transparency, enabling real-time tracking of products from raw material sourcing to end-of-life disposal.

**Consumer Engagement and Education**

Effective ERP implementation also relies on consumer engagement and education. Digital platforms can inform consumers about the environmental footprint of products, promoting recycling and sustainable consumption choices. These platforms can offer incentives for sustainable practices and provide practical information on participating in recycling programs.

**Future Directions**

The regulatory landscape continues to evolve, with initiatives like the GS1 Digital Link standard introduced in 2018 replacing traditional barcodes with QR codes by 2027 and the EU regulations for supply chain transparency and anti-counterfeiting introduced in 2019. These regulatory efforts not only ensured that Connected Packaging technologies met safety and quality standards but also promoted their adoption by providing a clear legal framework. As a result, companies were more willing to invest in these technologies, knowing that they were supported by robust standards and regulations.

The ongoing development of EPR (Extended Producer Responsibility) and DPP (Deposit-Return Packaging) frameworks also highlights the critical role of governance in driving innovation and adoption in the field of sustainable packaging and product responsibility. These early regulatory efforts set the stage for a more detailed discussion on regulatory and ethical considerations in Connected Packaging, underscoring the pivotal role of governance in fostering innovation and adoption.

Industry reports and forecasts from organisations like Allied Market Research, Mordor Intelligence, and Smithers project significant growth for the Connected Packaging market. According to Statistics MRC, the global

Connected Packaging market was valued at $46.59 billion in 2023 and is expected to reach $75.45 billion by 2030, growing at a CAGR of 7.1% during the forecast period. Furthermore, the 2024 Appetite Creative Global Connected Packaging Report surveyed 3,000 brand owners, finding that 88% of them plan to use Connected Packaging in 2024.

The key points from the Global Connected Packaging Summit in the summer of 2024 further reinforce the widespread interest and engagement in this field. The summit, which had over 500 registered attendees from across 43 different countries, showcased 18 speakers across 11 thought-provoking discussions and presentations, with the speakers answering over 60 live questions from the audience.

Experts highlighted the potential of connected packaging as a new media channel, allowing brands to bypass intermediaries and establish direct consumer connections. Successful implementations, such as those by Red Bull and Lego, demonstrate the power of user-generated content and community engagement. However, challenges like cost, technological adoption, and changing consumer behaviour require brands to be creative and agile in their approach.

Data analytics and insights emerged as crucial aspects of connected packaging. AI integration enhances data collection, providing valuable insights into consumer behaviour and product usage. Variable data printing (VDP) enables unique codes on products, supporting direct consumer interaction, product authentication, and personalised marketing. These technologies also contribute to sustainability efforts by reducing waste and optimising operations.

Product authentication remains a key driver for connected packaging adoption. Advanced technologies like digital fingerprints and invisible markers are being used to combat counterfeiting and protect brand integrity. Consumer engagement through connected packaging is evolving beyond simple data capture, with brands using it to educate consumers about sustainability and facilitate social impact initiatives.

The summit concluded that connected packaging is no longer an optional extra but an essential tool for authentication, marketing, and regulatory compliance in the modern business landscape.

## The Evolution Wave

Gartner's Hype Cycle provides a valuable framework for understanding the evolution of connected packaging technology. This well-known model describes the path that emerging technologies typically follow on their journey to mass adoption. The cycle consists of five distinct phases:

1. **Technology Trigger:** This initial phase occurs when a potential technology first sparks public interest and media attention.

2.  **Peak of Inflated Expectations:** In this phase, publicity reaches its zenith, often fuelled by early success stories, but also marked by some failures.

3.  **Trough of Disillusionment**: Interest begins to wane as implementations fail to deliver on overinflated promises. Many abandon the technology at this stage.

4.  **Slope of Enlightenment:** This phase sees a resurgence as the technology's benefits become more widely understood. Second and third-generation products emerge, improving upon earlier iterations.

5.  **Plateau of Productivity**: Finally, the technology reaches mainstream adoption. Clear criteria for assessing provider viability are established, and the technology's broader market applicability becomes evident.

In the context of connected packaging, industry experts have observed significant progress through these stages. Based on extensive work with brands across various industries, it's clear that connected packaging technologies are rapidly advancing through the Gartner Hype Cycle. Currently, the technology appears to be firmly on the 'Slope of Enlightenment,' with both brands and consumers recognising the tangible benefits.

As connected packaging approaches the **'Plateau of Productivity,'** we're witnessing increasingly sophisticated and user-friendly implementations that deliver real value. This marks an exciting time for the technology, as it transitions from a novelty to an essential tool for brand engagement and data collection. The progression suggests that connected packaging is poised to become a standard feature in the near future, offering substantial benefits to both brands and consumers.

This progression through the Hype Cycle reflects the maturing nature of connected packaging technologies. As the industry moves towards the Plateau of Productivity, we can expect to see more standardised best practices, improved ROI metrics, and wider adoption across various sectors.

I caught up with **Andrew Manly, Communications Director from the AIPIA** – (the Active & Intelligent Packaging Industry Association).

His take on Connected Packaging I think sits nicely here– "Active and Intelligent Packaging is one of the most exciting and potentially game-changing developments the packaging industry has seen in the last 50-60 years. It ranks up there with the blister pack, inkjet printing and multi-head weighing which all enabled the packaging industry to meet new demands from legislation, retailers and customers.

Smart Packaging is now ubiquitous in the apparel and clothing sector and meeting the challenges of counterfeiting in the luxury goods, wines and spirits and electronics sector. While it has gained huge traction in food & beverage and cosmetics it is still to break into mainstream, full-scale products. For pharmaceuticals, the needs for legislation and meeting the challenge of fake medicines and the need for better patient monitoring and compliance are leading to more and more investment in smart packaging technologies. There is a lot more scope for the adoption of smart packaging in all these sectors, but in the last decade the progress has been astonishing.

Today all innovative packaging developments have to be seen in the context of the sustainability issue. Recycling and environmental factors dominate the packaging agenda and mean, rightly or wrongly, that much of the budgets for new packaging are focused in that area. This has had an effect on investment on other packaging technologies, including smart packaging. Perversely smart packaging is already playing a major role in avoiding waste, particularly food waste. It is also helping to modernise and upscale recycling technologies through digital watermarks and AI-powered vision systems.

There is always talk of ROI and the facts show that Smart Packaging can deliver on several levels, such as reducing waste, consumer engagement, brand protection and awareness, tamper evidence, counterfeit protection and traceability. Those who look for Return on Investment should look closely at what these technologies can offer. One excellent example is the role Active Packaging can play in helping to preserve and protect perishable foods and so reduce waste and improve margins. If used effectively (and there is scant evidence of it currently) the bottom line performance for

Brand Owners and Retailers can be greatly enhanced – and help the environment too!

Improvements in Supply Chains is another critical factor where Smart Packaging is, and will, play a major role. At AIPIA we see this as a core element of the future success for the technologies, where traceability, serialisation, condition monitoring and shelf life extension can enable a new era of more efficient, transparent and effective supply chains, reducing costs and waste and therefore, hopefully improving trust and profitability along the value chain. To meet these needs the Association has assembled a major consortium of companies in the Smart Food Chain, bidding for EU funding to enable us to reinvent the food supply chain using smart technologies.

As for which technologies are winners and users? Well, these will be those which have established themselves in the minds of the consumer, such as the QR code, which is now fully accepted and is set to become a globally recognised standard with the advent of the GS1 Digital Link, with its multi-functional features. There are now billions of RFID/NFC tags on billions of packages, securing, informing and protecting the goods inside. Also, inventory management is now so much easier thanks to these tags, the right product in the right place at the right time! There is much more to come.

Finally, Smart Packaging is ushering in a new era of Big Data. The flows of data captured (in a responsible way) by smart packaging go both ways: to the consumer about the product, its provenance, authenticity and condition; to the retailer, Brand owner and logistics company about the consumer triggers, the supply chain performance and the effect of promotion campaigns – to name just a few. Part of the work AIPIA has to do is help companies understand how to use and share that data both internally and externally. It's a big job!

Active & Intelligent Packaging has taken enormous strides in the last decade. But it is not nearly where we in AIPIA and our members want it to be. There is much work still to do, not least in educating consumers about the benefits of these technologies and how to access them and use them effectively. The AIPIA Community was built to include all elements of the value chain, which includes those doing valuable research into new materials and combining smart features to be a TOTAL, not partial solutions. It is the only voice of the whole sector and, with the support of its members, will take on the challenges and help the industry and those who use it, grow and prosper."

# Chapter 2: The Technology Behind Connected Packaging

Connected Packaging is revolutionising how brands interact with consumers by integrating digital technologies into traditional packaging. This chapter delves into the various technologies that make Connected Packaging possible, exploring how they work, their applications, and real-world examples of their use.

## QR Codes and Barcodes

### How They Work

Barcodes and QR (Quick Response) codes are among the earliest technologies used in Connected Packaging.

- **Barcodes:** A barcode is a machine-readable representation of data, typically in the form of a series of parallel lines of varying widths and spacing. When scanned by a barcode reader, it translates the lines into data that can be used to identify products, track inventory, and manage supply chains.

- **QR Codes**: QR codes are two-dimensional barcodes that store information both horizontally and vertically. They can hold more data than traditional barcodes, including URLs, contact information, and text. Consumers can scan QR codes using smartphone cameras, which then direct them to digital content such as websites, product information, or promotional offers.

There is an industry-wide initiative to transition from limited 1D barcodes to the more data-rich and capable 2D barcodes, standardising their adoption across the supply chain to meet various stakeholder needs and enhance consumer engagement by 2027. Referred to by GS1 as the Sunrise project.

The project is focused on the transition from traditional one-dimensional (1D) barcodes, like EAN/UPC, to two-dimensional (2D) barcodes in the global supply chain.

**The key aspects of this project are:**

**1. Recognizing limitations:** Traditional 1D barcodes only hold basic product identification data, which is no longer sufficient for today's demands for detailed product information, traceability, and authentication.

**2. Adopting 2D barcodes:** 2D barcodes offer a solution as they can carry significantly more data, enabling supply chain stakeholders and consumers to access a wealth of additional product details.

**3. Industry-wide initiative:** The project, dubbed **"Sunrise 2027"**, is an industry-wide initiative to prepare for and implement the acceptance of 2D barcodes at points of sale (POS) and points of care (POC) by the year 2027.

**4. Standardisation and benefits:** By adopting 2D barcodes as a standardised solution, the project aims to address various needs such as improved inventory management, enhanced recall readiness, transparency into sustainability and ethical sourcing, better product authentication, and increased brand trust.

**5. Consumer engagement:** One key aspect is enabling consumers to access detailed product information, nutritional data, allergens, and sustainability details, and engage with web-based brand activities by simply scanning the 2D barcode with their smartphones, powered by GS1 Digital Link technology.

**6. Implementation support:** The project involves organisations like GS1 US providing guidance and support to brands, retailers, healthcare providers, and solution providers in migrating their systems and processes to accept and leverage 2D barcodes, ensuring a streamlined transition to the "next dimension" of barcodes.

To gain deeper insights into the role of GS1 standards in connected packaging, we spoke with **Camilla Young, Programme Lead-Next generation of barcodes at GS1 UK.** Her expertise sheds light on the importance of standardisation and the future of barcode technology.

### What role do GS1 standards play in enabling connected packaging solutions?

GS1 standards put the "connected" in connected packaging. We provide the necessary framework for consistency, interoperability and communication between systems and stakeholders, ensuring QR codes work throughout the supply chain, right up until they are scanned by consumers' phones. GS1 standards facilitate the integration of connected packaging experiences, by connecting the products unique identifier- the GTIN (Global Trade Item Number) with the digital ecosystem. Our standards ensure that QR codes used in packaging are compliant with GS1 requirements, which is crucial for ensuring they can be reliably scanned, and that data is provided in a consistent format for systems to accurately interpret.

### How does the GS1 Sunrise project contribute to supply chain visibility and traceability?

50 years after the introduction of the original barcode, GS1 is working with the industry across the world to prepare to begin scanning QR codes powered by GS1 at the checkout in 2027. In the UK we are working with industry to meet this goal and support the transition to this new smarter code.

There is an ongoing need for greater transparency and traceability throughout the supply chain to mitigate risks and improve customer service. While the ubiquitous linear barcode has served us well for the past 50 years, something more powerful is needed to meet the growing data demands of our hyper-connected modern world.

To meet these new demands, we, along with our GS1 colleagues around the world, are now actively collaborating with industry to support the global transition to QR codes powered by GS1. These new, smarter symbols not only store far more data than their linear predecessors, they can also be scanned by both smartphones and point of sale (POS) scanners.

This opens a whole new world of possibilities, providing all the information consumers and stakeholders across the supply chain need. The GS1 compliant syntax contained also enables crucial supply chain data such as expiry dates, batch numbers, pack dates and country of origin, to be encoded directly into the QR.

Stakeholders across the supply chain can then use this to more effectively track, trace and manage inventory and stock. Consumers can then scan the QR using their smartphone to access and engage with any product information they may require. There are some excellent case studies demonstrating the art of the possible here, from 'farm to fork' traceability of fish and fruit, to automated product recall processes.

Of course, traceability doesn't end once a product is consumed. Recycling and circular economy initiatives can be powered by GS1 standards, as serialised data can enable businesses to track every unique instance of a product or pack. There are some great examples of this from Co-op and Ocado who have been piloting use of QR codes powered by GS1 in conjunction with UV tagging to track plastic waste.

**What case studies demonstrate the successful implementation of GS1 standards in Connected Packaging?**

The global effort to make this vision for the future of retail a reality is now well underway we are already seeing several retailers running pilots, and brands scaling integrating with their connected pack strategies and 22 leaders from the world's biggest companies have signed a global joint statement calling for the transition to QR codes powered by GS1.

There are already lots of pilots and rollouts happening across the world, with use cases spanning consumer marketing, waste reduction, automated recalls, regulatory compliance, 'farm to fork' traceability, anti-counterfeiting, packaging circularity and accessibility to vital packaging information for blind and visually impaired consumers.

Some published information we recommend checking on the GS1 website

**Food waste reduction and safety:** Woolworths Australia seeing multiple benefits from 2D barcodes (gs1.org)

**Fruit traceability:** Citrus fruit traceability in a snap (gs1.org)

**Label less bottles**: Jeju SamDaSoo mineral water aiming for "top" levels of efficiency and sustainability (gs1.org)

**Packaging re-use**: Coca-Cola's reusable, refillable bottles benefit from innovative QR Codes powered by GS1

Camilla Young's insights underscore the critical role that GS1 standards play in enabling connected packaging solutions and improving supply chain visibility. The Sunrise project she describes represents a significant step forward in barcode technology, with far-reaching implications for both businesses and consumers.

However, it is important to note that 2027 is not going to have a radical flash moment of change, there will likely be a very long transition period and for now, QR codes will co-exist along barcodes for some time. Retailer will need to upgrade their hardware and software for a full changeover.

Building on this foundation of standardised, data-rich QR codes and barcodes, connected packaging opens up a vast array of possibilities for brands to engage with consumers, streamline operations, and create innovative experiences. Let's explore the diverse applications of connected packaging technology, each demonstrating its potential to revolutionise consumer-brand interactions, supply chain management, and marketing strategies.

**Applications of Connected Packaging**

This comprehensive list covers a wide range of use cases, from providing detailed product information to enabling personalised marketing campaigns. Throughout this book, we'll delve into real-world examples of these applications, showcasing how brands are leveraging connected packaging to create value and enhance customer experiences. Let's begin by examining some key areas where connected packaging is making a significant impact:

1. **Product Information**:
   - Provide detailed product specs, ingredients, and nutritional facts
   - Offer interactive usage instructions and video tutorials
   - Link to allergen information and dietary guidelines
2. **Loyalty Programs**:
   - Implement digital loyalty schemes
   - Reward customers for repeat purchases and engagement
   - Track and manage customer points or rewards through the packaging
3. **Instant Win Promotions**:
   - Incorporate exciting gamification elements
   - Offer immediate prizes to boost interaction and sales
   - Create scratch-and-win style digital experiences
4. **Authentication**:
   - Combat counterfeiting by allowing consumers to verify product authenticity
   - Implement blockchain-based verification systems
   - Provide real-time authentication results
5. **Accessibility**:
   - Offer alternative ways to access product information for users with visual or auditory impairments

- ○ Implement technologies like NaviLens for enhanced accessibility
- ○ Provide multi-language support for diverse user groups

6. **Sustainability Information:**
   - ○ Communicate eco-friendly initiatives
   - ○ Provide detailed recycling instructions
   - ○ Showcase the brand's environmental impact and goals

7. **Product Origin and Traceability:**
   - ○ Allow consumers to trace the journey of products from source to shelf
   - ○ Provide information on sourcing practices and fair trade initiatives
   - ○ Offer real-time updates on product location and estimated delivery (for e-commerce)

8. **Personalised Content:**
   - ○ Tailor content to individual preferences and demographics based on user data
   - ○ Offer personalised product recommendations
   - ○ Provide customised usage tips and tricks

9. **Marketing Campaigns:**
   - ○ Engage consumers with promotional content
   - ○ Run QR code-based contests and sweepstakes
   - ○ Offer exclusive digital content or experiences

10. **Supply Chain Management:**
    - ○ Track products through the supply chain
    - ○ Ensure accurate inventory management
    - ○ Reduce losses and improve efficiency

11. **Augmented Reality Experiences:**
    - ○ Create interactive AR product visualisations
    - ○ Offer virtual try-on experiences for cosmetics or apparel
    - ○ Provide immersive brand storytelling

12. **Customer Feedback and Surveys:**

- o  Collect real-time feedback on products
- o  Conduct market research through interactive surveys
- o  Gather valuable consumer insights

13. **Social Media Integration**:
- o  Enable easy sharing of product experiences on social platforms
- o  Create shareable branded content or filters
- o  Run social media-based contests or challenges

14. **Product Reordering**:
- o  Implement one-click reordering through packaging scans
- o  Set up subscription services for consumable products
- o  Provide easy access to compatible products or accessories

**QR Codes and Barcodes**

## Understanding the Types of QR Codes in Packaging

QR codes (Quick Response codes) have revolutionised packaging by enabling direct interaction between consumers and products through smartphones. They come in various types, each serving different purposes from basic information retrieval to enhanced security features. Here, we explore the 5 types of QR codes used in packaging:

### 1. Static QR Codes

Standard QR codes are the most basic form, typically encoding static information such as URLs, text, or simple instructions. They are cost-effective and easy to implement, making them widely used for basic consumer engagement purposes. However, they cannot be updated. Once created, the information encoded in a static QR code cannot be changed.

This means if there are updates or corrections needed to the content (such as URL changes or revised contact details), a new QR code must be generated and distributed.

**Limited Tracking and Analytics:** Static QR codes do not provide detailed analytics or tracking capabilities. Unlike dynamic QR codes that can capture data on scans, location, and user behaviour, static QR codes offer no insights into how or where they are scanned.

**Less Flexible:** Due to their fixed nature, static QR codes are less adaptable to dynamic needs. For instance, if a promotional campaign requires rotating content or time-sensitive information, static QR codes would not be suitable without frequent regeneration.

**Obsolescence**: If the information encoded in a static QR code becomes outdated or obsolete, it can lead to confusion or frustration for users who scan it expecting current information.

## 2. Dynamic QR Codes

Dynamic QR codes differ from static ones in that they can be edited or updated after creation. This flexibility allows brands to change the encoded content without needing to reprint the QR code itself. It's particularly useful for campaigns where information or promotions need to be updated regularly. These are much more useful than the static brother or sister mentioned in number 1.

## 3. Serialised QR Codes

Serialised QR codes are unique codes generated for each individual product within a batch or production run. Each QR code links to specific information about that particular item, such as manufacturing details, batch numbers, or even personalised content. This level of granularity aids in product traceability and authentication.

## 4. SKU-Level QR Codes

QR codes can also be implemented at the SKU (Stock Keeping Unit) level, linking directly to product-specific information such as ingredients, nutritional facts, or usage instructions. This type of QR code enhances consumer convenience by providing detailed and relevant information at the point of sale.

## 5. Secure QR Codes

Secure QR codes incorporate additional layers of protection to prevent tampering or unauthorised access. They often use encryption techniques to safeguard sensitive information encoded within the QR code. Secure QR codes are crucial for applications requiring data integrity and consumer privacy, such as in pharmaceuticals or high-value goods.

**Choosing the Right QR Code for Your Packaging**

Selecting the appropriate QR code type depends on the specific goals and requirements of your packaging strategy:

- **Campaign Goals**: Determine whether you need a static QR code for consistent information or a dynamic QR code for updates.
- **Product Specificity**: Consider whether serialised or SKU-level QR codes are necessary for detailed product information or traceability.

- **Security Needs**: Evaluate if secure QR codes are essential to protect sensitive data or maintain brand integrity.

## Case Studies and Examples

### Case Study 1: Serialized QR Codes in Pharmaceuticals

### Revolutionising Cannabis Packaging with Digital Innovations

In recent years, advancements in digital packaging technology have catalysed transformative changes across industries like pharmaceuticals and cannabis. Companies such as ePac have pioneered innovative solutions that not only enhance regulatory compliance but also bolster consumer safety and marketability.

Ryan Kelly, previously Director of Market Development at ePac, highlighted the pivotal role of connected packaging in revolutionising the cannabis sector. Through ePac Connect, each pouch is assigned a unique digital identity via QR codes, facilitating seamless tracking from production through to sale. This technology not only ensures strict adherence to regulatory standards but also empowers consumers with crucial product information accessible through a simple scan.

In a notable pilot program in Switzerland, ePac deployed ePac Connect for managing adult-use recreational cannabis. The Unique QR codes on each pouch link consumers to comprehensive details including chemical composition and batch history, fostering transparency and aiding regulatory bodies in enforcing consumption limits effectively.

Beyond regulatory compliance, ePac Connect serves as a powerful tool for consumer engagement. Consumers can access product-specific information, discover community initiatives, or participate in loyalty programs, all through a quick QR code scan. This dual-functionality not only meets regulatory requirements but also cultivates brand loyalty and enhances consumer satisfaction in a competitive market.

Kelly emphasised the broader implications of connected packaging, envisioning its adoption beyond cannabis to industries like pharmaceuticals. He drew parallels with medications using serialised QR codes to provide patients with detailed dosage instructions, expiration dates, and links to personalised medical information.

In summary, ePac's innovative approach to cannabis packaging signifies a significant shift towards enhanced consumer safety, regulatory compliance, and market competitiveness. Technologies like ePac Connect set a precedent for integrating smart packaging solutions that improve product integrity and consumer engagement across diverse industries. (You can read more about this particular case study on the Appetite Creative YouTube Channel and The Global Connected Packaging Summit - 2023.)

**Benefits of Serialised QR Codes in Cannabis Packaging:**

1. **Enhanced Traceability:** Serialised QR codes enable precise tracking of each product from cultivation to consumption, ensuring transparency and accountability throughout the supply chain.
2. **Improved Consumer Safety:** Access to accurate dosage and usage information directly from the packaging promotes safe and responsible use of cannabis products.
3. **Regulatory Adherence:** Compliance with stringent regulatory standards is facilitated by providing verifiable data on product authenticity, quality, and compliance.

ePac Flexibles' use of serialised QR codes exemplifies how smart packaging technologies can enhance transparency, consumer safety, and regulatory compliance in the cannabis industry and beyond.

### Loyalty Programs: Vital Strategies in the Modern Business Landscape

In today's fiercely competitive market, brands are constantly innovating to foster customer loyalty and drive sales amidst unprecedented inflation. Loyalty programs have emerged as crucial tools in achieving these objectives. This chapter explores their pivotal role, spotlighting the success of Appetite Creative's program, which boosted sales by 28% in the food and beverage sector within six months. It also examines how QR codes and smart packaging, exemplified by Pepsi's 50% increase in first-party data over 18 months, integrate seamlessly into loyalty strategies.

### The Essential Role of Loyalty Programs

Loyalty programs have long been essential for retailers, amplified by research showing they can increase revenue by up to 75%. These programs not only boost spending but also enhance customer satisfaction and retention, vital in a global industry worth millions of dollars. Statista claims that a recent study revealed 7 out of 10 customers prefer digital discount coupons so it makes sense that Connected Packaging can help streamline that.

### Impact of Inflation on Consumer Behaviour

As inflation rises, consumers face financial strain, impacting industries like food and beverage. These challenges have intensified with the pandemic, digital shifts, and low unemployment rates.

**Loyalty Programs as Cornerstone Strategies**

Amid these challenges, loyalty programs stand out as cornerstone strategies for brands, particularly in food and beverage. Appetite Creative's success underscores their effectiveness, with half of Americans now viewing these programs as essential.

**Navigating Challenges of Devalued Programs**

Despite their potential, loyalty programs must offer genuine value. Many consumers would abandon programs lacking benefits, requiring brands to manage them carefully for mutual benefit.

**Smart Packaging and QR Codes: Enhancing Connectivity**

Smart packaging and QR codes have revolutionised loyalty programs by offering seamless, connected experiences. Smart packaging integrates technology into product design, offering benefits like freshness indicators and interactive features. QR codes, meanwhile, provide access to digital content, promotions, and loyalty rewards, enhancing consumer engagement.

**Harnessing Connected Packaging for Loyalty**

By combining smart packaging with QR codes, brands create interactive experiences within loyalty programs. These include exclusive offers, real-time product information, personalised rewards, and direct feedback channels, enriching customer satisfaction and retention.

**Pepsi's Data-Driven Success**

Pepsi's strategy exemplifies this approach, achieving a 50% increase in first-party data through QR codes and loyalty programs. This data-driven insight enables Pepsi to tailor offerings and drive growth.

The loyalty program can be activated through interaction, behaviour or purchase depending on the type of QR and plan put in place. It is up to the brand to decide what is feasible based on their packaging and manufacturing, current printing set up and the aims and goals of the programme.

**Dynamic QR Codes in Retail**

The benefit of the dynamic code is that content can be changed regularly for seasonality and real-time updates. Dynamic QR codes on product labels to update promotions and discounts in real-time. This approach enhances consumer engagement by offering current information directly accessible via smartphone scanning.

Dynamic QR codes are increasingly being used in various industries for marketing, customer engagement, and operational efficiency. Here are a few more examples of how dynamic QR codes are utilised:

1. **Starbucks**: Starbucks uses dynamic QR codes in their mobile app for payments and loyalty rewards. Customers can pay for their orders and earn points by scanning the QR code displayed on their smartphone at checkout. The QR code dynamically updates with the customer's payment and loyalty information.
2. **McDonald's**: McDonald's has integrated dynamic QR codes into their marketing campaigns. For instance, they have used QR codes on packaging to provide nutritional information, promotions, and interactive games. These QR codes can be updated in real-time to reflect current offers or seasonal promotions.
3. **IKEA**: IKEA uses dynamic QR codes on their products and in-store displays to provide additional product information, assembly instructions, and design inspirations. Customers can scan the QR

codes to access relevant content that is regularly updated based on current inventory and promotions.

4. **Airbnb**: Airbnb utilises dynamic QR codes for enhanced security and convenience in their digital check-in process. Hosts and guests can use the Airbnb app to generate and scan QR codes for keyless entry to rental properties, ensuring a seamless and secure experience.

5. **Uber**: Uber integrates dynamic QR codes into their ride-sharing platform for safety and verification purposes. Drivers and passengers can scan QR codes within the Uber app to confirm the ride details, ensuring that both parties are matched correctly and enhancing safety during pickups.

## Printing your QR code

As we've explored in previous chapters, connected packaging offers numerous benefits for brands and consumers alike. However, one of the biggest challenges in realising these benefits is the actual implementation of QR codes or other connected elements onto packaging. This process can involve either significant changes to artwork or additional printing stages in the production process. Let's examine the key considerations and solutions for this challenge.

### Approaches to QR Code Implementation

When considering QR code implementation, brands need to carefully evaluate their data tracking needs versus the investment required:

1. **Serialised Approach**
   - Enables rich product digital tracking
   - Requires adapting packaging lines for inline printing

- Offers more advanced capabilities for loyalty programs and instant win promotions

2. **Basic QR in Artwork Files**
   - Easier implementation
   - Enables tracking at the SKU level
   - May be sufficient for initial connected packaging efforts
   - Limited functionality for loyalty programs and instant win promotions

The choice between these approaches often depends on the brand's specific goals, budget, and existing production capabilities.

1. **Static QR Code**

   The simplest approach is to include the same QR code across all packaging for a product line or SKU. This static QR code is incorporated into the packaging artwork itself. While easy to implement, this limits the data tracking to the SKU level rather than capturing information at the individual package level.

2. **Serialised QR Codes**

   For more granular data tracking, brands can print a unique, serialised QR code on each individual package. This allows capturing data points tied to that specific package rather than just the SKU. Serialised QR codes require inline digital printing capabilities to generate the codes during the packaging run.

3.  **Batched QR Codes**

    A middle ground is to use the same QR code for a particular
    production batch, then change to a new code for the next batch.
    This enables tracking at a batch level while avoiding the complexity
    of serialising every single package.

The difficulty and cost increase from a static QR code to serialised package
printing, including the QR in the artwork file, is straightforward for printers.
Serialisation requires an inline digital printer integrated with coding
software and databases to generate the unique QR codes systematically.

The two leading suppliers of inline coding and printing systems for
packaging lines are Koenig & Bauer and Domino. Koenig & Bauer offers
several digital printer models that can print QR codes, barcodes, text and
graphics at various speeds. Domino's range includes ultra-high resolution
inkjet printers capable of printing detailed QR codes.

## Digital Printing Solutions for Connected Packaging

Digital printing technologies have revolutionised the packaging industry,
offering numerous advantages over traditional printing methods. These
benefits are particularly relevant for connected packaging applications,
where flexibility, customisation, and data integration are crucial. Let's
explore the key advantages of digital printing solutions:

1.  **Reduced Time** Digital presses significantly reduce changeover
    time compared to analogue printing. This is especially critical when
    managing multiple short-run and time-critical printing jobs, a
    common scenario in connected packaging projects.

2. **Reduced Waste** Digital printing requires less material preparation than analogue methods. Traditional printing involves greater waste for short runs due to plate setup and cleaning for every change or error modification. In contrast, digital presses need only one make-ready for all versions when printing multiple SKU jobs.

3. **Reduced Cost** Compared to conventional analogue printing, digital presses facilitate cost reduction by eliminating the need for costly printing plates. They typically use less paper/packaging and ink than traditional methods. Additional cost savings can be achieved through reduced energy consumption, especially when compared to traditional methods requiring arc drying lamps.

4. **Increased Capacity** By using digital presses for short-run work, converters can free up substantial capacity on conventional presses for long-run jobs. This results in an overall capacity gain that exceeds the capacity of the digital press alone.

5. **Labour Reallocation** Traditional printing methods require highly skilled workers with specific training, who are increasingly difficult to recruit as older generation workers retire. Digital presses are typically easier to operate and can be run by multi-skilled staff. This reduces reliance on a shrinking labour pool and allows converters to redeploy labour to other value-added services, as the machines can work with limited manual intervention.

6. **Agility** The ability to produce short-run packaging quickly and cost-effectively offers converters the agility required to better respond to market trends and position themselves to meet their brand customers' requirements. Digital presses allow the incorporation of flexo stations: flood primer, spot varnish, and embellishment functions, among others, can be included for a new print job, and a single operator can still run the press.

**Key Players in Digital Printing for Connected Packaging**

While several companies offer digital printing solutions, two major players stand out in the variable data printing space for packaging:

1.  Koenig & Bauer
2.  Domino Printing Sciences

Both Koenig & Bauer and Domino provide comprehensive solutions, including not just printers, but also the necessary inks, software, and services for QR code printing on packaging. The choice between providers typically depends on specific production requirements such as print quality, speed, package materials, and data tracking needs.

By understanding these implementation approaches and available technologies, brands can effectively leverage QR codes to enhance consumer experiences, streamline operations, and build stronger connections with their customers. Whether opting for a serialised approach with inline digital printing or incorporating basic QR codes into existing artwork, the key is to align the implementation strategy with overall business objectives and operational capabilities.

As we move forward, we'll explore how brands are using these technologies to create innovative applications in connected packaging, demonstrating the real-world impact of overcoming these implementation challenges.

# KOENIG & BAUER

**Koenig & Bauer Coding Technologies** is a leading supplier of printing presses and coding solutions for packaging. Their digital printing systems are designed to integrate seamlessly into packaging lines for online printing of variable data like QR codes.

Alphajet Printers The Alphajet series from Koenig & Bauer includes compact inkjet printers capable of printing QR codes, barcodes, text, and graphics at speeds up to 300 metres/min. The non-contact digital printing uses solvent-based or UV-curable inks suitable for coding onto various packaging materials.

## Webcol Digital Printers

For higher resolution printing, Koenig & Bauer offers the Webcol line of drop-on-demand UV inkjet digital printers. The Webcol 76D model can print high-quality QR codes, graphics, and text at resolutions up to 720 x 720 dpi directly onto packaging surfaces.

All Koenig & Bauer printers integrate with their coding software for generating serialised or batched QR codes from central databases. This enables track and trace at a package or batch level.

A groundbreaking project is emerging from Koenig & Bauer AG, tentatively named "Follow." This innovative solution promises to revolutionize the packaging industry by seamlessly integrating various stakeholders and technologies.

Koenig & Bauer's new Connected Packaging app aims to create a unified ecosystem for printing companies, brands, and consumers. This comprehensive platform offers a wide array of features, including:

- Ingredient and dietary requirement identification
- Augmented reality experiences
- Product traceability
- Authentication solutions
- Interactive campaign competitions
- Tracking capabilities
- AI-powered data analysis

What makes this project particularly intriguing is the central role of printing companies in facilitating these connected packaging experiences. By bridging the gap between manufacturers and consumers, "Follow" has the potential to transform how we interact with packaged products.

To gain more insight into this exciting development, I had the opportunity to speak with Sandra Wagner, VP Digitalization and the project director. Our conversation shed light on the vision and potential impact of this innovative solution.

**How does the "follow" platform integrate with existing printing technologies and workflows?**

Follow is a stand and agnostic alone platform - existing printing technologies and workflows will not be affected. It was important for us to create a product, which will not interfere with existing technology and software and will be used as a useful add-on.

**What specific benefits does "follow" offer to brand owners in terms of consumer engagement and data insights?**

Mainly it's about getting consumers connected with the product and the real package. Aside from websites and other marketing channels like social media - Follow offers for brands the possibility to connect consumers directly with their products. In short: Follow enables the package to act as a new channel of communication - even as a screen, whether at home or at the store.

Data insights are provided as well and give Brandowners the possibility to get direct Consumer insights - is the product easy to use or do the consumers like the package, how much are they interested in sustainability information just to name a few examples. Aside from the classical Data insights like Scan Rates, Geolocation etc. are also available - of course, based on GDPR.

## How does the platform address sustainability concerns in packaging?

There are several angles to this - either sustainability information like $CO^2$ footprint of the package, or depending on the Brandowner decisions - further information like special sustainability campaigns, advice for recycling and so on.

Nearly all information which is beneficial for consumers and brands can be shown via Follow on the package or linked to landing page, social media or other channels.

## How does "follow" ensure data privacy and security for both brands and consumers?

Follow is strictly based on GDPR regulations, no data will be shared or tracked without permission of the Brands or the consumers.

This was one of our main goals - to build a solution which is absolutely secure and compliant and ensure that data protection and transparency about data handling is fully available to every user.

## What are the key challenges brands might face when implementing this technology, and how does Koenig & Bauer address them?

Key challenges might be to add Follow as a new Brand ambassador tool and marketing channel, this needs some adjustment in marketing strategy and planning. The possibilities with Follow are enormous and finding the right Use Cases for the brand or the specific SKU is key. Here we help with knowledge on how to start with Follow, how to find the right Use-Case as well as checking metrics if the campaign is successful and how the campaign and experience can be improved.

**How does the platform's augmented reality feature enhance the consumer experience?**
Augmented Reality is very beneficial when it comes to experiences like gamification or tutorials.
It can be greatly used for collecting AR motives, Scavenger hunts etc.
The main benefit is it can enhance the package in size and can be changed anytime. AR can be placed around the package, with even more motives or information. Independent from the physical package this content can be changed or replaced anytime - which gives totally new possibilities for the complete life-cycle of the product especially in terms of marketing and engagement.

**How does "Follow" compare to other connected packaging solutions in the market?**
Follow is the only end-to-end solution in the market. From the packaging layout until the recycling offers Follow provides the full transparency and possibility through the whole life-cycle of a package.

**What future developments or features are planned for the "follow" platform?**
Recycling and Logistics is a field where we are analysing new features for Follow right now.

**How does the platform support personalisation and customisation of consumer experiences?**

With AR inside Follow the consumer can easily personalise their package. Imagine buying a box of chocolate for your loved ones and put via AR a personal message on the box.

This is possible with serialised codes in combination with Follow and offers completely new ways of personalisation - and this works two ways!

Think about: you have special dietary needs - with this technology, the brand can help you to eat more healthily - very important when it comes to Diabetes or similar dietary needs.

It's a true personal connection between consumer to consumer or brand to consumer.

**How does the platform support multi-channel marketing strategies?**

In Follow you can easily link to landing pages, social media etc. We see Follow as a new marketing channel, but linked to all existing channels. It´s not replacing other channels, it´s a new channel for marketers with link to the real product. Due to Follow Technology it´s the a multichannel tool in it´s core.

**Domino Printing Sciences** is a major player in the variable data printing space for packaging, providing end-to-end coding and marking solutions.

Domino Printing Sciences provides end-to-end coding and marking solutions, offering a range of products suitable for connected packaging applications:

### a) K600i Inkjet Printer

- Domino's flagship inkjet printer
- Capable of printing QR codes, graphics, and data at ultra-high resolutions up to 1,200 dpi
- Uses Domino's piezo-electric ink technology for crisp, readable QR codes suitable for scanning

### b) V230i Thermal Inkjet (TIJ)

- Suitable for lower resolution coding at higher speeds
- Can print QR codes, barcodes, and text at line speeds up to 600 metres/min
- Ideal for fast packaging lines

### c) Software Integration

- Domino's QuickDesignApp and EditApp software integrate with the printers

- Enables generation of variable QR codes from central databases or ERP systems
- Facilitates serialised or batched QR printing for connected packaging applications

One notable case study from Domino demonstrates the potential of digital printing for connected packaging. In this example, Domino's technology was used to implement variable pricing on packaging. This innovative approach allows brands to dynamically adjust prices based on factors such as demand, inventory levels, or promotional strategies, all without the need for reprinting entire packaging runs. This level of flexibility and responsiveness is a game-changer in the packaging industry, offering new possibilities for pricing strategies and market adaptability.

**Revolutionising Food Safety: Thailand's 7-Eleven Intelligent Barcode Initiative**

In a groundbreaking move to enhance consumer safety and streamline operations, GS1 Thailand has spearheaded an innovative intelligent barcode system across the nation's vast network of over 12,000 7-Eleven convenience stores. This cutting-edge project, focusing on the popular ready-to-eat food product range, marks a significant leap forward in retail technology and food safety management.

At the heart of this initiative lies the sophisticated GS1 DataMatrix, a two-dimensional barcode capable of encoding crucial product information. Each DataMatrix contains three vital pieces of data:

1. Global Trade Item Number (GTIN)
2. Best before date
3. Batch/lot number

Ready-to-eat food product with GS1 DataMatrix. Image from GS1 Thailand.

This wealth of information, compactly stored within a single scannable code, enables real-time tracking and verification of product freshness at the point of sale (POS).

**Innovative Coding and Marking Techniques:** The implementation employs a dual approach to product marking, tailored to different packaging materials:

1. Thermal Transfer Overprinting (TTO): Used for flexible packaging materials, providing high-quality, durable prints.
2. Thermal Inkjet (TIJ): Applied to more rigid surfaces, offering fast, high-resolution coding.

These advanced marking technologies ensure clear, long-lasting codes that maintain readability throughout the product's lifecycle.

The primary objective of this ambitious project is to create an impenetrable safety net, preventing the sale of expired ready-to-eat products. By implementing this system, 7-Eleven Thailand aimed to significantly reduce food safety risks, enhance customer trust, and set a new standard for quality control in the convenience store industry.

The scope of this initiative is truly comprehensive, encompassing not only all 7-Eleven retail outlets but also extending to the brand's manufacturing facilities. This end-to-end integration ensures a seamless flow of accurate product information from production line to store shelf, creating a robust and transparent supply chain.

As Thailand's 7-Eleven stores embrace this intelligent barcode system, they're not just improving food safety – they're pioneering a new era of smart retail, where technology and consumer well-being intersect to create a superior shopping experience. The combination of advanced coding techniques and comprehensive data management sets a new benchmark

for food safety and traceability in the convenience store sector.

**Key Benefits and Operational Improvements:**

1. **Enhanced Food Safety:** Real-time expiration tracking significantly reduces the risk of selling outdated products.
2. **Reduced Food Waste:** Accurate inventory management and timely sales of near-expiry items minimize unnecessary waste.

3. **Streamlined Operations:** Elimination of manual price reduction processes frees up staff time for customer service and other valuable tasks.

4. **Improved Inventory Accuracy**: Automated tracking provides real-time insights into stock levels and product lifecycles.

5. **Cost Savings:** Reduction in labour costs associated with manual price adjustments and inventory checks.

6. **Enhanced Customer Trust:** Consistent quality assurance builds consumer confidence in product freshness and safety.

7. **Data-Driven Decision Making**: Detailed product data enables more informed choices in purchasing, stocking, and promotions.

8. **Compliance Assurance:** Automated systems help ensure adherence to food safety regulations and standards.

9. **Supply Chain Visibility:** Improved traceability from manufacturer to point of sale enhances recall effectiveness if needed.

10. **Environmental Impact:** Reduction in food waste contributes to sustainability efforts and reduces environmental footprint.

This comprehensive approach not only addresses immediate food safety concerns but also delivers a wide range of operational and strategic benefits. By leveraging advanced technology, 7-Eleven Thailand is setting a new standard for efficiency, safety, and customer service in the convenience store industry.

I spoke with two experts from Domino Printing Sciences. **Craig Stobie, Global Director of Strategic Sectors** with over 28 years at the company, **and Nigel Allen, Marketing Manager for 2D Codes & High Resolution Inkjet,** shared their insights.

Their combined experience offers a unique perspective on the evolution and current trends in connected packaging technologies.

**How has digital printing technology evolved in recent years within your company?**

Digital printing is a game-changer in the world of packaging and labels. While traditional printing processes still hold value, the rise of digital printing offers exciting possibilities for customisation, speed, and cost savings. As technology continues to advance, digital printing is set to shape the future of packaging and labels, helping converters to stand out in a competitive market. For more than a decade Domino have developed a range of mono digital bars that complement a traditional analogue flexo press as well as a comprehensive range of Digital Colour presses for packaging and corrugates.

**Can you describe your most innovative digital printing product and its unique features?**

- Domino's new N730i digital colour label press, which is based on its latest state-of-the-art Generation 7 Technology platform, is the product of more than 40 years of inkjet innovation, including

- i-Tech ActiFlow

  - Ink is continually re-circulated within the print bar and through the print head modules - delivering consistent print colour and superior reliability

- i-Tech CleanCap

  - Print nozzles are purged to ensure optimal print quality and reliability

- i-Tech StitchLink

  - Automated print head alignment for accurate registration and ease of set up

**How are you addressing environmental concerns in your digital printing technologies?**

Digital printing helps tackle many of the environmental concerns around packaging as you can print short runs exactly to order rather than mass produce labels and packaging, transport them to a warehouse and then dispose of what you don't use. Digital printing allows a just-in-time approach to be implemented

**What industries or applications have shown the most growth for digital printing?**

Label Converter market and FMCG have all embraced the change to digital and the benefits of digital

**How do you see artificial intelligence and machine learning impacting digital printing in the near future?**

Improvement in workflow and artwork generation. AI will help provide more efficiencies for just in time production

**What challenges do you foresee for the digital printing industry in the next 5-10 years?**

The change in adopting digital printing and moving away from analogue technologies

**How are you addressing the increasing demand for personalisation and variable data printing?**

Digital printing can accommodate print-on-demand and short-run changes as it requires minimal set-up and creates minimal substrate wastage, thereby maximising productivity

**Can you discuss any recent breakthroughs in ink technology for digital printing?**

An increased focus on sustainability and the relationship between links and the evolution in packaging materials

**How do you balance the need for speed with print quality in your digital printing solutions?**

With speeds of up to 250 metres per minute , Domino digital devices are designed to fit seamlessly into production environments

**What advancements have you made in integrating digital printing with finishing and converting processes?**

Domino digital devices are designed to fit into an analogue printing process to add the ability to print variable date. Domino's unique intelligent i-Tech system and ink container replacement, ensures simple operation for this digital inkjet printer. Options include a roller section or complete web extension section, enabling simple integration of this digital inkjet printer into an existing machine

Variable data printing onto a range of coated and uncoated substrates

**What role does digital printing play in the growing packaging and label markets?**

The introduction of digital inkjet print technology has without doubt been invaluable for label and packaging printers. And those businesses that have been open to adopting innovation and introducing new digital inkjet technologies are the ones that maintain competitive advantage by meeting increasing customer demands for 'what they want, when they want it' output, while improving efficiency, managing costs and delivering on sustainability. When it comes to label and packaging printing, there are many advantages to digital inkjet printing compared to other methods

**How are you addressing colour consistency and colour management challenges in digital printing?**

The importance of colour in product packaging cannot be over-emphasised. The N610i provides brand owners and designers the scope to create designs with a far wider colour gamut cost-effectively. Our seven colour press can achieve in excess of 92% of the Pantone® colour range without the need to make plates or the complexity of mixing spot colours. Lightfastness is a property of the ink colourants that describes how permanent, and thus resistant to fading, when they are exposed to UV radiation. Lightfastness indicates the suitability of the ink to be used in different applications, with those aimed for outdoors use and long-term direct sun exposure requiring very good resistance to fading and higher level of the lightfastness. Measured using the Blue Wool Scale, a widely adopted standard used to express the lightfastness of pigments and dyes, the Domino UV90 ink set achieves the highest possible score of eight across a range of substrates, offering the maximum resistance to fade within the industry

**Can you discuss any collaborations or partnerships that have driven innovation in your digital printing offerings?**

Since 2015 Domino has been part of the Brother Industries group which has provided access to further expertise in digital print

**How do you see the relationship between offset and digital printing evolving in the coming years?**

Domino product scan be added to traditional analogue presses allowing the variable data/ digital element to be added to maximise their original investment. Once the Flexo press needs replacing, Domino has an excellent range of digital colour presses which can fill the void

## What steps are you taking to improve the durability and longevity of digitally printed materials?

Lightfastness - This is a property of the ink colourants that describes how permanent, and thus resistant to fading, they are when exposed to UV radiation. Lightfastness indicates the suitability of the ink to be used in different applications, with those aimed for outdoors use and long-term direct sun exposure requiring very good resistance to fading and higher level of the lightfastness. Measured using the Blue Wool Scale, a widely adopted standard used to express the lightfastness of pigments and dyes, the Domino UV90 ink set achieves the highest possible score of eight across a range of substrates, offering the maximum resistance to fade within the industry

## How are you addressing the need for faster turnaround times in the printing industry?

Complete workflow automation removes the need for operator intervention and allows full integration into your Management Information System (MIS). It also provides seamless integration with the Esko Automation Engine via the Print-to-Digital Press Module

## What advancements have you made in substrate compatibility for digital printing?

Domino has a number of test centres throughout the world that are continually evaluating new development in packaging and inputting the results into the R& D teams at Brother and Domino to ensure our products and inks quality.

## How do you see digital printing technology contributing to the concept of Industry 4.0 or smart factories?

While all manufacturers would welcome the ability to maximise OEE and reduce waste, for some, the outlay on new Industry 4.0 equipment may seem to carry too high a risk without guaranteed return on investment. This may be particularly true for SMEs with limited capital expenditure and dated legacy equipment, especially given current socio-economic circumstances. Domino have developed a range of offerings to make the transition easier.

Servitisation – where clients pay for an outcome or service rather than directly purchasing equipment – may offer a compelling solution to this problem. Indeed, servitisation is starting to gain international recognition by organisations, including the World Economic Forum, as a viable way of increasing economic productivity and contributing positively to global decarbonisation efforts. Suppliers who offer manufacturing solutions as part of a servitisation model have a vested interest in ensuring that these products are kept running efficiently and consistently over time – maximising performance while minimising wastage.

Within Industry 4.0, servitisation means manufacturers work with a partner who can offer support-as-a-service in line with their specific goals, such as increasing uptime, throughput, and/or quality. Such a model not only passes the outcomes-focused risk on to the supplier but also assists with cost by allowing the investment to be spread out over a period of time in an OPEX rather than a CAPEX model. Moreover, with such service-based contracts, clients can embrace a land, adopt, expand, renew (LAER) approach to their investment. This allows for change and flexibility when outcomes or goals change while remaining at the forefront of innovation with access to new technology as it becomes available.

**Conclusion**

In conclusion, digital printing solutions have emerged as a cornerstone of connected packaging applications, offering a range of benefits that are transforming the industry. These technologies are enabling brands to create more engaging, efficient, and data-driven packaging solutions, with advantages that include:

- Reduced production time and material waste

- Increased capacity for personalisation and variable data

- Greater agility in responding to market demands

- Enhanced ability to implement complex connected packaging features

Interestingly, we're seeing traditional printing companies heavily expanding into this space, offering extended services beyond just printing. This shift indicates several important trends:

**1. The growing importance of connected packaging in the broader packaging industry**

**2. A recognition that brands need comprehensive, end-to-end solutions rather than just printing capabilities**

**3. The convergence of digital technologies and traditional printing expertise**

This expansion of services by printing companies demonstrates their commitment to staying relevant in a rapidly evolving digital landscape. It also suggests that connected packaging is not just a passing trend, but a fundamental shift in how brands interact with consumers and manage their supply chains.

As the industry continues to evolve, we can expect to see even more innovative applications of digital printing in connected packaging. From advanced product authentication measures to hyper-personalised consumer experiences, the possibilities are vast. The key for brands will be to strategically leverage these technologies to create packaging that not only protects and presents their products, but also serves as a powerful tool for engagement, data collection, and brand storytelling.

Looking ahead, the integration of digital printing and connected packaging technologies promises to blur the lines between physical and digital brand experiences, opening up new frontiers in marketing, supply chain management, and consumer interaction. As these technologies become more sophisticated and accessible, they will undoubtedly play a crucial role in shaping the future of packaging and brand communication.

### Near-Field Communication (NFC)

While digital printing solutions have revolutionised the implementation of QR codes and variable data on packaging, they are just one part of the connected packaging ecosystem. As brands seek to create even more interactive and seamless experiences for consumers, they are turning to additional technologies that complement and extend the capabilities of printed elements.

One such technology that has gained significant traction in recent years is Near Field Communication (NFC). Unlike QR codes, which require optical scanning, NFC tags use short-range wireless technology to communicate with smartphones and other NFC-enabled devices. This technology opens up new possibilities for brand-consumer interactions, offering unique advantages in terms of user experience and data security.

In the next section, we'll explore how NFC tags are being integrated into packaging designs, the benefits they offer, and the innovative ways brands are using this technology to enhance their connected packaging strategies. From simple tap-to-learn product information to sophisticated authentication and loyalty programs, NFC is pushing the boundaries of what's possible in packaging interactivity.

### What is NFC?

NFC technology enables short-range communication between compatible devices. NFC tags embedded in packaging can be read by smartphones with NFC capabilities, allowing for instant interaction without the need for an app or internet connection.

The Near Field Communication (NFC) market has seen substantial growth in recent years, with projections indicating continued expansion. Valued at $15.5 billion in 2019, the market is expected to reach $54.5 billion by 2028, growing at a compound annual rate of 14.8% from 2021 to 2028. This growth is largely driven by the increasing adoption of mobile commerce, the development of wearable technology, and the technology's enhanced security features and ease of use.

The proliferation of NFC-enabled smartphones has been a significant factor in the technology's widespread availability. As of 2019, over 2 billion NFC-enabled devices were in use globally, making the technology accessible to a large portion of the world's population. This accessibility has opened up new possibilities for NFC-embedded packaging interactions.

Contrary to previous misconceptions, NFC chips and tags have become increasingly affordable to manufacture. Production costs have drastically reduced due to technological advancements, with tags now available for less than $0.05 per unit when purchased in large quantities. This cost reduction has made NFC technology feasible for a broader range of products, including those in lower price brackets.

NFC in packaging offers numerous applications, from monitoring food freshness and detecting tampering to combating counterfeiting. However, its potential for marketing and brand engagement is particularly noteworthy. NFC-enabled packaging can provide consumers with product information, special discounts, social media links, usage instructions, and various interactive experiences.

## Uses in Connected Packaging

- **Product Authentication:** NFC tags can verify the authenticity of products, helping to combat counterfeiting. Consumers can tap their smartphones against the NFC tag to confirm the product is genuine.

- **Consumer Engagement:** NFC tags can provide a wealth of information and interactive content. For example, an NFC-enabled wine bottle could offer tasting notes, vineyard information, and food pairing suggestions when tapped with a smartphone.

- **Loyalty Programs**: Brands can integrate NFC into loyalty programs, allowing consumers to earn points or rewards by tapping their phones against the product packaging.

## Case Study - with Johnnie Walker

Johnnie Walker has leveraged NFC technology to offer consumers immersive digital experiences. For instance, their limited edition Johnnie Walker Blue Label Cities of the Future bottles come with NFC tags that, when tapped, allow consumers to explore a virtual version of Singapore in the year 2220. This experience, created by digital artist Luke Halls, can be accessed by consumers visiting a Lotte Duty-Free store at Changi Airport in Singapore. They can explore a futuristic Singapore brought to life through

digital content on their mobile devices, complemented by a pop-up installation of LCD displays in the retail outlet. This initiative not only enhances consumer engagement but also showcases the potential of combining physical and digital realms.

**Leaders in NFC for Connected Packaging**

Several companies have emerged as leaders in NFC technology for connected packaging. Among these, Avery Dennison and Atma.io stands out for its innovative solutions and recent developments.

 **Avery Dennison**, a global leader in materials science and manufacturing, has been at the forefront of smart packaging solutions, particularly in RFID (Radio-Frequency Identification) and NFC (Near Field Communication) technologies. Founded in 1935, the company has evolved into a multinational corporation with operations in more than 50 countries. Avery Dennison specialises in the design and manufacture of a wide range of labelling and functional materials, including pressure-sensitive adhesive materials, RFID inlays, and speciality medical products.

The company's innovative approach to smart packaging has positioned it as

a key player in the digital transformation of supply chains and retail experiences. Their RFID solutions enable improved inventory accuracy, enhanced supply chain visibility, and more efficient omnichannel retail operations. Meanwhile, their NFC technology applications facilitate consumer engagement, product authentication, and interactive marketing campaigns.

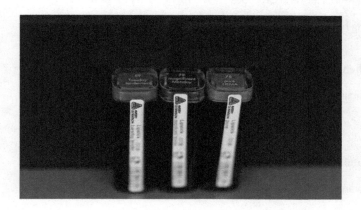

# atma.io
## by Avery Dennison

In 2021, the company launched Atma.io, a connected product cloud platform within its Intelligent Labels business segment. Atma.io positions itself as a comprehensive connected product platform, offering an ecosystem of applications that create and manage unique digital identities for everyday items, providing a single source of truth that unlocks value across the entire product lifecycle for brands, supply chains, and consumers alike.

Atma.io represents a significant advancement in connected packaging:

**Digital Identity:** The platform assigns unique digital identities to physical items, enabling brands to track products throughout their lifecycle.

**Technology Integration:** Atma.io leverages various tagging technologies, including RFID, NFC, and QR codes, providing flexibility for different packaging needs.

**Comprehensive Functionality:** The platform offers solutions for supply chain visibility, inventory management, product authentication, and consumer engagement.

**Sustainability Focus**: A key feature of Atma.io is its ability to help brands track the environmental impact of their products, aligning with growing consumer demand for sustainable practices.

**Cross-Industry Application:** Atma.io's solutions are used across various sectors including retail, food and beverage, and pharmaceuticals.

Drive world class consumer experiences with NFC + atma.io and Appetite Creative

The introduction of platforms like Atma.io demonstrates the evolution of NFC in connected packaging from simple authentication and engagement tools to comprehensive solutions that address multiple aspects of product lifecycle management and brand-consumer interaction.

For the purpose of this book **Tom Duncan, Global Director of Connected Packaging at Avery Dennison,** provided valuable insights into the future of connected packaging, discussing the role of technologies like NFC and RFID, changes in consumer-brand interactions, and Avery Dennison's vision for smart supply chains and the Internet of Things.

**How do you envision the role of technologies like NFC and RFID evolving in the connected packaging space?**

Making products and packaging 'connected' via digital identification technologies such as RFID, NFC and QR codes mean they can be managed and tracked via data platforms. This helps to identify and eliminate 'black holes' in inventory, reduce dwell times in warehouses and optimise distribution. It also means stock takes can be completed in minutes and hours versus days and weeks, ensuring that the right product is available at the right time, in the right place. Revealing valuable new information can help brands differentiate their products with consumers such as providing carbon footprint data and information on ethical sourcing of raw materials. Combining these digital identification technologies creates mutual benefits. Retailers and their supply chain partners get complete real-time inventory visibility on every unique item or batch of items, helping to inform business decisions. Meanwhile, consumers can scan the QR code with their smartphone to get the story or history of every unique product.

**How do you think connected packaging will change the way consumers interact with brands?**

If we take cosmetics and beauty as an example, brands in this space want to ensure transparency, supply chain optimisation and effective management of expiry dates with high accuracy. Small items such as makeup are well suited to RFID tagging. Interactive elements can be added to the packaging, enhancing the consumer experience beyond the capabilities of a barcode. Cosmetics and beauty consumers particularly care about the ingredients and origins of their items. RFID, NFC and QR codes can all help convey this information which provide brands with interactive features that their customers will enjoy. Additionally, when consumers know exactly what items are made of and how to recycle them it encourages circularity. This points to a future where more and more consumers and brands embrace packaging as an interactive communication tool, rather than viewing it as merely a means to carry their goods during transit and provide basic information about the product.

**What is Avery Dennison's long-term vision for the role of connected packaging in the broader context of smart supply chains and the Internet of Things (IoT)?**

Connected products are critical to enabling a circular economy. While we see elements of reuse and recycling today, the coming years will take this to a new level. Much of this is mandated by legislation which will necessitate far greater transparency of products and the materials or ingredients they are made of. The most advanced initiatives fall under the European Union 'Green Deal' — this includes the Digital Product Passport scheme, which is part of the Ecodesign for Sustainable Products Regulation (ESPR). Rolling out from 2027, the initial focus is on the EV batteries and textile sectors but will also affect the ecosystem around it such as logistics and retailers. The whole purpose of the scheme is to consider the entire life-cycle of products, from production to end-of-life disposal, covering all the processes relating to materials sourcing, production and end-of-life disposal. It will require a deep level of transparency from producers (and their suppliers) as to exactly where all constituent materials are sourced and will necessitate digital identification along every step of the journey. Connected packaging will help adhere to the EU's Packaging and Packaging Waste Regulation (PPWR). For example RFID embedded connected packaging would enable more accurate and efficient sorting of waste, leading to increased reuse and recycling rates. The ability to track products and packages across their lifecycle can also help support the deployment of EPR (Extended Producer Responsibility) systems, which are critical to the implementation of PPWR.

**NFC V QR codes**

Connected packaging is revolutionising consumer-product interactions, with QR codes and NFC (Near Field Communication) leading the charge. Both QR codes and NFC technologies have their distinct benefits, but it's crucial to weigh the cost versus the benefits.

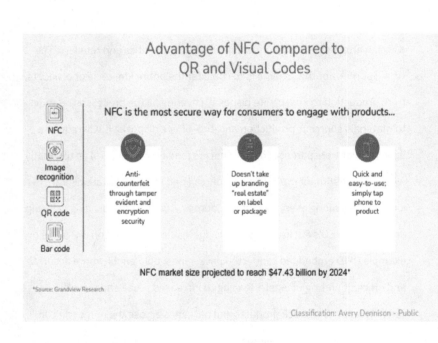

## QR Codes: Accessible and Cost-Effective

QR codes are ubiquitous two-dimensional squares that can be scanned by smartphones. Their popularity and effectiveness in connected packaging stem from several key factors:

**Universal Compatibility:**

- Readable by nearly all modern smartphones without additional apps
- Works across iOS and Android platforms

2. **Cost-Efficiency:**

- Inexpensive to generate and print
- No additional hardware required for implementation

3. **Versatility:**

- Can encode various types of data: URLs, plain text, contact info, etc.
- Scalable to fit different packaging sizes

4. **Easy Generation and Management:**

- Numerous free and paid tools available for QR code creation
- Can be easily updated (by changing the linked content) without altering the code itself

5. **Marketing Potential:**

- Can be integrated into packaging design for aesthetic appeal
- Enables trackable marketing campaigns

6. **Data Capacity:**

- Can store significant amounts of information (up to 4,296 alphanumeric characters) o Different versions available for varying data needs

7. **Error Correction:**

   o Built-in error correction allows successful scanning even if partially damaged

8. **Customisation Options:**

   o Can include logos or colours while maintaining functionality
   o Design flexibility to match brand aesthetics

9. **Analytics Integration:**

   o Easy to track scans and user engagement
   o Provides valuable data for marketing insights

10. **Consumer Familiarity:**

   o Widely recognised and understood by consumers
   o Lower barrier to engagement compared to newer technologies

These features make **QR codes** a highly accessible and cost-effective solution for brands looking to implement connected packaging strategies. Their simplicity and widespread adoption continue to make them a popular choice across various industries.

| Advantages | Challenges |
|---|---|
| Universal Accesibility | Limited data capacity |
| Cost-effectiveness | Internet dependency |
| Versatility in content delivery | Security concerns(spoofing, malware) |
| Easy implementation | |

## NFC: Dynamic and Secure

Near Field Communication (NFC) is a short-range wireless technology that allows data exchange between devices in close proximity, typically within a few centimetres. Unlike QR codes, which are static and can be scanned from a distance, NFC offers a more dynamic and secure method of interaction.

## Key Features of NFC:

1. **Proximity-based Activation:** NFC requires devices to be in close contact, usually within 4 cm, enhancing security and reducing the risk of unintended interactions.

2. **Two-way Communication:** Unlike QR codes, NFC allows bidirectional data transfer, enabling more complex interactions between devices.

3. **Dynamic Content:** NFC tags can be rewritten, allowing for real-time updates and personalised experiences.

4. **Enhanced Security:** NFC employs encryption protocols, making it more secure for sensitive transactions like payments.

5. **No App Required:** Most modern smartphones have built-in NFC capabilities, eliminating the need for a separate app to scan codes.

6. **Multiple Data Types:** NFC can transfer various types of data, including URLs, contact information, and even trigger specific actions on devices.

7. **Power Efficiency:** NFC tags are passive and don't require a power source, making them cost-effective for large-scale deployment.

| Advantages | Challenges |
| --- | --- |
| High data capacity | Higher implementation costs |
| Instantaneous interaction | Limited device compatibility |
| Enhanced security | |
| Offline functionality | |

## Choosing the Right Technology

The decision between QR codes and NFC depends on several factors:

**1. Content requirements:** NFC for extensive content, QR for simpler interactions

**2. Budget constraints:** QR codes for cost-effectiveness, NFC for premium experiences

**3. User experience:** NFC for instant, offline interaction; QR for broad accessibility

**4. Security needs:** NFC for enhanced security

| Aspect | QR Codes | NFC |
| --- | --- | --- |
| Functionality | Visual, scannable by most smartphone cameras | Wireless, short-range communication, requires NFC-enabled devices |
| User Experience | Requires opening camera app and aiming | Often just requires tapping phone to package |
| Data Capacity | Can store more data, especially in complex versions | Limited data storage, but can link to online content |
| Cost | Inexpensive to implement, just printing costs | Higher cost due to embedded chips and integration |
| Security | Can be easily replicated, lower inherent security | More secure, harder to clone, can include encryption |
| Updateability | Static once printed, but can link to dynamic content | Can be rewritable, allowing for content updates |
| Analytics | Scan data available through linked platforms | Can provide more detailed interaction data |
| Consumer Adoption | Widely recognized and used | Growing adoption, but less familiar to some consumers |
| Environmental Impact | Minimal additional impact on packaging | Adds non-recyclable elements to packaging |
| Marketing Potential | Versatile for various campaigns, visible marketing tool | Enables more seamless and interactive experiences |

As I emphasised in a recent article, **"The key is to align the chosen technology with the specific needs of the product and the budget constraints of the business."**

Both QR codes and NFC offer unique advantages in connected packaging. The choice depends on the product, target audience, and budget. Regardless of the technology chosen, connected packaging has the potential to create immersive and memorable consumer experiences, enhancing brand loyalty in an increasingly digital marketplace.

The choice between NFC and QR codes often depends on the specific product, target audience, budget, and desired customer experience. Some brands are opting to use both technologies to maximise reach and functionality.

As NFC technology continues to evolve, and the cost continues to come down, it's clear to me that it will play an increasingly important role in connected packaging strategies. The high level of brand interest and perceived consumer demand indicate that NFC and QR codes are likely to become a standard feature in packaging across various industries in the near future. Whether or not it will be the right choice for a pack of crisps or a carton of juice I have my doubts but, expect to see a growth in their use and applications.

**Bluetooth Beacons and RFID**

**Functionality**

- **Bluetooth Beacons**: These small, battery-powered devices use Bluetooth Low Energy (BLE) to broadcast signals that can be detected by nearby smartphones. When a consumer's phone comes within range, it can trigger a notification or action, such as displaying a promotional message.

- **RFID (Radio-Frequency Identification)**: RFID uses electromagnetic fields to automatically identify and track tags attached to objects. RFID tags consist of a small chip and an antenna, and they can be either passive (powered by the reader's signal) or active (battery-powered).

# How Does RFID Work?

**Step 1**
RFID tag preparation and placement

**Step 2**
RFID reader activation

**Step 3**
Tag activation and powering

**Step 4**
Tag response

**Step 5**
Data capture by RFID reader

**Step 6**
Data processing and integration

**Step 7**
Inventory management and checkout process

## Applications

- **Retail Environments:** Bluetooth beacons can enhance the shopping experience by sending personalised offers and product information to consumers' smartphones as they move through the store.

- **Inventory Management:** RFID tags are widely used in supply chains to track products in real-time, improve inventory accuracy, and reduce shrinkage.

- **Interactive Displays RFID:** Enabled packaging can trigger interactive displays in retail settings, providing additional information or promotional content when a product is placed near the display.

**Case Study**

Levi's used RFID technology to streamline its inventory management. By attaching RFID tags to its clothing, the company improved inventory accuracy, reduced out-of-stock items, and enhanced the overall efficiency of its supply chain.

Additionally, Levi's launched BOOST (Business Optimization of Shipping and Transport), an AI- and machine learning-driven e-commerce solution designed to optimise inventory management and streamline order fulfilment. When consumers find an item out of stock online, BOOST can locate nearby stores carrying the item, broadening the search for available products. This system not only improves operational efficiency and reduces costs but also provides consumers with a better shopping experience. BOOST accounts for about 40% of eligible e-commerce orders and is expected to handle 100% by Black Friday, with plans to expand globally.

**Augmented Reality (AR)**

- Augmented Reality (AR): AR overlays digital content onto the real world through a smartphone or AR glasses. AR-enabled packaging can transform a product into an interactive experience. For example, a cereal box might turn into a 3D game or animation when viewed through a smartphone app.

- **Enhanced Consumer Interaction:** AR can create immersive brand experiences. Imagine scanning a soda can to see a virtual character come to life and tell the brand's story, or using AR to visualise how a piece of furniture would look in your home.

- **Data Collection and Insights**: Both AR and digital watermarking can provide brands with valuable data on how consumers interact with their products. This data can be used to refine marketing strategies, improve product design, and enhance the overall consumer experience.

What follows are some of the top augmented reality (AR) companies and their notable case studies in Connected Packaging:

 **1. Zappar** is an XR service provider and a pioneer in the world of augmented reality (AR) and connected packaging solutions. Their XR platform and services allow brands to enhance product packaging with immersive, digital experiences accessed through smartphone cameras.

A major trend Zappar has focused on is WebAR, which enables AR experiences to be activated by simply scanning a QR code through a mobile web browser, without requiring an app download. This frictionless access drives higher adoption among consumers.

According to research reports AR can deliver a scan rate between 2-4% for CPG brands, as well as 90+ seconds average dwell time, and around 2.9 scans per user. AR advertising outperforms traditional advertising by 55% dwell time, and around 2.9 scans per user. Based on the study's benchmarking, users reported levels of 'happiness' and 'surprise' that were 55% higher for AR campaigns compared to standard (non-AR) advertising scans per user. This suggests significant engagement and positive reception of AR-enhanced packaging.

Furthermore, the study indicates that consumer packaged goods (CPG) brands adopting AR in their packaging campaigns could potentially achieve a 3% growth in market share. This finding underscores the effectiveness of augmented reality in driving consumer interest and market performance for brands in the FMCG sector.

Zappar has worked with big brands like Nestle, Unilever, Bombay Sapphire, and Chiquita on innovative connected packaging campaigns. One of the first examples of this in the industry is Zappar's work with Bombay Sapphire, allowing customers to scan the bottle for cocktail recipe videos and product storytelling. For Nestle's cereal brands, Zappar's WebAR experiences unlocked engaging brand partner promotions tied to popular franchises like Avatar: The Way of the Water, Jurassic World, DC Super Heroes and The Lion King.

Zappar also collaborated with Chiquita Bananas on an AR experience that brought the brand's story of sustainably sourcing and supporting farmers in their supply chain to life for consumers.

For Zappar connected packaging is most successful when it evolves beyond one-off marketing campaigns. They envision an "always on" strategy where QR codes are permanently integrated into packaging to continuously refresh AR content over time based on seasonal promotions, new product information, etc. Some brands like Coca Cola, Ab in Bev, Unilever and Nestle are already executing this vision.

Overall, with the benefits AR can bring across retail strategies Zappar believes connected packaging that blends physical products with digital AR experiences will become a "corporate imperative" for brands.

As CEO Caspar Thykier states, connected packaging surrounds us in our everyday lives. It's on our kitchen tables, on our desks at work, in our kids' school bags. The humble pack is a brand's most vital communications channel but until now it's been sitting there silently. Now, thanks to the ever present smartphone and the power of Zappar's augmented reality platform, product packaging can be transformed into a multimedia portal that can deliver value to both the consumer and the brand.

### - Case Study: Zappar- Sesame Street

Zappar collaborated with Just Play to develop a captivating WebAR (Web-based Augmented Reality) experience aimed at enriching online customer interactions. The goal was to replicate the engaging 'try me' feature found in stores, enhancing it with an innovative twist. Using augmented reality, users could superimpose their child's head onto various characters, allowing them to explore and interact by mimicking storied roars and stomping together.

## 2. Blippar

Blippar was founded in 2011, arguably the first pioneer in this space.

As early as 2015, Heineken launched an innovative campaign to communicate its commitment to sourcing 50% of its hops and barley from sustainable sources by 2020. This campaign showcases how connected packaging and augmented reality can be used effectively to engage consumers with sustainability initiatives.

**Campaign Overview:**

**Theme:** Celebrating farmers who grow Heineken's ingredients

**Technology:** Blippar mobile app (augmented reality)

**Interactive Elements:** Scannable Heineken bottles and beer mats

**Key Features:**

**The 'Legendary 7' Animation:** A 60-second Wild West-style animation featuring seven real farmers from the UK, Netherlands, France, Germany, and Greece who produce sustainable hops and barley

**In-Depth Farmer Stories:** Detailed content about each farmer's sustainable practices. For example, Jacky Brosse's beehives in his barley fields in France

**Sustainability Information:** Details about Heineken's broader sustainability commitments

**Consumer Engagement:** Users could create and share selfies - 7elfie – to show support for the farmers

**Offline Integration:** Poster executions in the style of Wild West "Wanted" posters to boost awareness

## Strategic Approach:

Mark van Iterson, Heineken's global head of design, explained the rationale: **"Sustainability is often seen to be complex and inaccessible for consumers. However, sustainability is at the heart of all that we do and we wanted to find a way to encourage consumers and all our stakeholders to easily engage with our Brewing a Better World programme."**

## Innovation in Sustainability Communication:

The campaign, titled "Legendary 7," aimed to challenge traditional sustainability reporting methods. By using augmented reality and interactive storytelling, Heineken made its sustainability efforts more engaging and accessible to consumers

## Key Takeaways:

Technology Integration: The use of Blippar's AR technology transformed static packaging into an interactive platform for storytelling

**Humanising Sustainability:** By focusing on individual farmers, Heineken personalised its sustainability efforts, making them more relatable to consumers

**Multi-Channel Approach:** The campaign effectively combined digital interaction with traditional advertising methods

**Consumer Participation:** Encouraging users to create and share content increased engagement and social media visibility

**Brand Alignment:** The campaign's Wild West theme creatively aligned with Heineken's brand image while delivering a serious message about sustainability

### 3. Wikitude

- Case Study: Wikitude developed an AR app for Patrón Tequila that enabled users to scan bottles and learn about the brand's history, production process, and cocktail recipes

### 4. Aircards

- Case Study: Air Cards created an AR experience for Strongbow cider bottles, allowing consumers to scan the label and play an interactive game

### 5. Augment

Case Study: Augment worked with Purina to create an AR experience for their pet food packaging. Customers could scan the package to see a 3D model of the product and access additional information

These are just a few examples, but many AR companies are actively exploring and developing innovative solutions for Connected Packaging, enabling brands to engage with consumers in new and interactive ways. One of the biggest advancements in AR is the ability to be able to launch a good level of Augmented Reality in the web browser without the need for a downloaded app. This became a game changer for Appetite Creative and we started using AR in our campaigns for gamification and fun selfie experiences.

**Digital Watermarking**

This technology embeds invisible codes into packaging that can be detected by a smartphone camera. Unlike QR codes, digital watermarks do not alter the visual appearance of the packaging. They can be used to provide additional product information, verify authenticity, or link to digital content.

Digital watermarking technology is a much-talked-about innovation. Digital watermarks can be applied to nearly any object or media, linking product packaging, print, or audio to interactive online content when scanned with an enabled device. These watermarks can be overt or covert and are read by mobile devices, computers, inspection system cameras, retail scanners, among other systems.

**Use Cases**

**Serialized Packaging**: Digital watermarks can contain serialised data, allowing for greater product traceability across the global supply chain. This enables consumer brands and food manufacturers to mitigate risks and gain real-time insights into product locations such as warehouses or distribution centres.

**Brand Protection**: Overt or covert digital watermarks can be added to products, packaging, labels, and product images. This helps brands identify and take action against counterfeit products that damage brand reputation and endanger consumer safety.

**Commercial Print**: Digital watermarking can transform static print media, such as brochures, posters, signage, and in-store print, into dynamic interactive point-of-sale (POS) materials. This creates an omnichannel experience for consumers by seamlessly integrating physical and digital content. It must be noted that the consumer must download an app to be able to allow the phone's camera to recognise the watermark.

**Sustainability**: Digital watermarks on product packaging can improve sorting at plastic waste facilities, preventing a large percentage of plastics from ending up in landfills. The HolyGrail 2.0 plastic recycling project is pioneering the use of digital watermarks for a circular economy, enhancing the sorting rates and recyclability of plastics.

**Digital Images & Documents:** Digital image and document watermarking help companies identify unauthorised use of digital assets. By combining digital watermarking with other technologies, brands can track and trace sensitive image and document leaks to the source, maintaining control over where digital assets are used and stopping unwanted distributions.

**Digital Watermarking**

Digital watermarks are imperceptible codes, roughly the size of a postage stamp, that can be embedded into the artwork or plastic of packaging. These watermarks can carry a wide range of data about the packaging, such as manufacturer, SKU, plastic type, food vs non-food use, etc.

The digital watermarking approach, by enabling much more precise sorting of packaging waste, aims to produce higher-quality recycle streams to boost plastics recycling in the circular economy. Currently the drawback for consumers on digital watermarking is they can't see it or need an app to interact with it so its biggest use is within the recycling and identification of waste.

The biggest company in this space is **Digimarc.**

Digimarc is known for its Digimarc Barcode, which allows efficient product identification and enhanced consumer engagement through the use of imperceptible digital watermarks. Digital watermarking is the science of hiding data in physical or digital objects in a way that is undetectable to humans but can easily be detected and read by machines.

With nearly 30 years of expertise and claims to have over 800 patents, Digimarc is certainly currently the biggest player in this space and is deeply involved in The Digital Watermarks Initiative HolyGrail 2.0, driven by AIM (European Brands Association) and powered by the Alliance to End Plastic Waste, is aiming to prove the viability of using digital watermarks to enable accurate sorting of packaging waste for more efficient and higher-quality recycling.

The initiative has developed prototype sorting systems that use high-resolution cameras to detect the digital watermarks on packaging as it moves along the sorting line. Based on the encoded data in the watermark, the systems can then sort the packaging into the appropriate streams (food vs non-food, plastic-type, etc).

I had the opportunity to ask Digimarc a few questions for this book. I asked **Riley McCormack, Digimarc President and CEO**

**How is digital watermarking contributing to sustainability initiatives within the packaging industry?**

Digimarc, the pioneer and global leader in digital watermarking technologies, and Wipak, a leading provider of flexible packaging solutions for global markets, recently announced a strategic partnership to help retailers and global brands embrace an eco-friendly strategy to product packaging. By combining Digimarc digital watermarks and Wipak's printed film technology, the companies help food, medical device, and pharmaceutical companies achieve sustainability and profitability goals through innovative packaging designed to advance the fight against plastic pollution and speed the path to net zero.

Together we are designing packaging for recycling and reuse, contributing to our goal of a circular economy. Digimarc Recycle represents a revolution in the sortation and recycling of plastic waste, allowing companies to progress against ever-increasing stakeholder demands for action on sustainability while addressing regulatory requirements such as the Packaging and Packaging Waste Regulation (PPWR) in Europe.

To provide greater context for the role of digital watermarking technology, Digimarc Recycle works by linking covert digital watermarks (used to deterministically identify plastic packaging to any desired level of granularity) applied to plastic packaging with an extensible cloud-based repository of product attributes, including packaging composition, food or non-food grade plastic, product variant, brand, SKU, and more. By integrating Digimarc digital watermarks into Wipak printed films, this revolutionary technology overcomes the limitations of current optical sorting technologies, significantly improving the quality and quantity of recycled materials while revealing invaluable and never-before-seen post-purchase product journey data.

Digital watermarking is a proven and high-ROI solution to the plastic pollution crisis, and it is available today. If we want producers to buy recyclate instead of continuing to use virgin plastic, we must improve the quality and quantity of plastic output at recycling facilities and offer a real opportunity for closed-loop recycling. Together with Wipak, we address this need – helping global brands and manufacturers get into action with the sustainable packaging and innovative technology required to effect environmental change, increase profitability, and unlock an immensely valuable source of new data.

**Ken Sickles, Digimarc's Chief Product Officer** answered my question- **What innovative projects or collaborations is your company currently involved in that you believe will set the standard for the industry?**

Digimarc, the pioneer and global leader in digital watermarking technologies, and OMRON, a leading provider of industrial automation solutions, recently announced a strategic partnership to take industrial automation solutions to a new level. The combination of Digimarc digital watermarks with OMRON machine vision technology represents an innovative approach to digital product identification and a transformative new force in industrial automation. Together, the companies are helping manufacturers and brands stay ahead of the competition, adapt to changing market conditions, and meet the increasingly stringent requirements of sustainable, customised products.

Advancements in industrial automation are critical to business operations and the safety of consumers. For example, labelling mix-ups have caused food products to be shipped without proper disclosure of ingredients. In the case of allergens like peanuts, milk, or gluten, this can be life-threatening. Manufacturers and brands require automated control and quality checks to prevent incorrectly matched parts.

Digimarc and OMRON have modernised industrial automation so manufacturers can now prevent mismatched components or mislabelled products, increase the speed and efficiency of the production process, and streamline the distribution and fulfilment of packaged goods. The solution also facilitates the recovery, sorting, and recycling of packaging materials post-use, reducing waste leaking into the environment and improving the quality and quantity of post-consumer recyclate.

This powerful combination of industrial automation expertise and advanced digital watermarking technology introduces a fully integrated solution to modernise industrial facilities.

Beyond industrial automation, Digimarc digital watermarks add value throughout the product lifecycle, enabling brands to address future challenges and meet consumer expectations with minimal additional investment. Once applied, digital watermarks automate the identification of packaging collection and sortation at material recycling facilities (MRFs) while generating sustainability metrics. Additionally, Digimarc digital watermarks support product authentication, dual-factor customer loyalty programs, next-generation retail checkout, and other enterprise applications, providing accretive value.

**Dom Guinard, Digimarc's VP of Innovation** then shed some light on future trends when I asked- **What future trends do you foresee in the connected packaging industry, and how are you (DigiMarc) preparing to meet those trends?**

The transition from 1D barcodes to 2D codes in preparation for Sunrise 2027, provides an unprecedented opportunity for brands and retailers to engage directly with customers. Brands need a direct-to-consumer (DTC) engagement channel, but consumers also demand it. Good news: QR code adoption has skyrocketed worldwide to facilitate both needs. This opportunity comes with a responsibility to convey true and accurate information. Which leads to an interesting and important trend among brands and retailers. The conversation is shifting from "I need a QR code" to "I need a digital identity for my products."

If all a brand needed was a QR code, it could get it from one of the numerous platforms offering QR codes: QR Monkey, QR Tiger, and more. However, the 2D revolution is more than snapping a QR code on a package or a simple change of data carrier. Companies now understand that the shift to 2D is an opportunity to digitise products, quite literally turn them on with digital identities. Beyond consumer engagement, digital identities are an entry point for countless services and use cases on the Web. When paired with a digital twin as part of an enterprise platform like Digimarc Illuminate, digital identities enable brands to fast-forward regulatory compliance, optimize context-aware marketing campaigns, access real-time product data, extend the life of products through resell and ecommerce programs, manage item serialisation and traceability, and address major issues like brand protection and plastic recycling.

**How do you envision the integration of digital watermarking with other emerging technologies, such as AI and blockchain, in the realm of connected packaging?**

Related to integrations with blockchain, Digimarc completed its second Digital Product Passport (DPP) pilot, conducted in collaboration with IOTA, the EU Blockchain Pre-Commercial Procurement project, and the Agro2Circular (A2C) EU project, to address challenges in recycling plastic in agri-food. The goal of the successful DPP pilot was to facilitate the recycling and upcycling of plastic used in the agricultural sector by providing digital identities and traceability data.

**What are some of the most exciting developments in digital watermarking technology that you believe will impact the future of packaging?** I asked **Tom Benton, Digimarc's Chief Revenue Officer**

As our world becomes increasingly digital, Digimarc maximises how products and multimedia can digitally interact with the various systems surrounding them. Digimarc's technology represents a step change in state-of-the-art digital watermarking proven in the fight to end plastic pollution, deter counterfeiting, protect content creators and consumers, revolutionise industrial automation, and transform how brands and consumers interact. Digimarc's technology uniquely connects physical and digital assets and delivers the same powerful capabilities across both domains.

Through Digimarc's Centre of Expertise program, premier-level members exclusively benefit from the ability to offer customers the option to deploy digital watermarks now and activate them later. Unlike other data carriers, which can't be turned off once deployed, Digimarc digital watermarks allow companies to anticipate future needs, while taking advantage of packaging refreshes, regional rollouts, marketing campaigns, and other product digitisation initiatives. For instance, companies can now ensure product packaging is recycle-ready in anticipation of upcoming regulations like the European Union's Packaging and Packaging Waste Regulation (PPWR).

A relatively new player, but gaining traction rapidly in this space is Polytag.

 **Polytag**: Offers comprehensive digital watermarking solutions for product authentication and supply chain management.

The "Polytag EcoTrace" program represents a game-changing approach to tracking single-use plastic recycling through the use of digital watermarking. Major brands and businesses across the consumer packaged goods industry are joining forces to fund and deploy this innovative solution.

Digital watermarking involves applying special UV-reactive fluorescent ink "tags" to product packaging labels during the standard printing process. These invisible tags essentially act as unique digital watermarks for each product's barcode. While unseen by the human eye, the UV tags can be detected and decoded by specialised detection equipment installed at recycling facilities.

Several major UK brands are already pioneering this technology. The Co-op has been using Polytag's UV tagging on their own-brand water bottles for over a year to gain insights into recycling rates. Other retail giants like Ocado and Aldi have also utilised the UV digital watermarking solution during trials.

The industry-led "EcoTrace" program aims to scale this up by strategically installing Polytag's UV detection units at the highest-volume recycling sites across the UK. With financial contributions from participating businesses, the plan is to achieve over 90% coverage of the total domestic plastic recycling throughput.

Locations already committed to deploying the detection equipment include recycling centres operated by major waste handlers like Biffa, Bryson, and Re-Gen Waste. The Welsh government has also pledged funding to ensure UV detection coverage at sites across Wales.

By unlocking real-time data on their packaging barcodes being recycled, brands can finally gain transparency into the recycling "black box" and develop informed strategies to improve circularity and meet environmental targets. The digital watermarking approach provides measurable, item-level recycling rates to verify recyclability claims and optimise sorting processes.

This cross-industry collaboration, enabled by Polytag's pioneering digital watermarking solution, is poised to drive a data-led revolution in boosting plastic recycling rates across the UK. A network of UV-tag detection equipment across 40+ UK sites will achieve over 90% coverage of the total domestic recycling throughout.

I had a conversation with **Alice Rackley - CEO and Co-founder at Polytag Limited** for the purpose of this book and she was able to give some really interesting insights.

### What future trends do you foresee in the connected packaging industry, and how are you (Polytag) preparing to meet those trends?

There is so much opportunity within the connected packaging space, particularly with the wide-spread adoption of GS1 standards. Polytag is an approved GS1 partner because we know that if everyone is 'talking the same language' there are many ways to innovate across the connected packaging ecosystem. Of course, QR codes on pack offer amazingly rich D2C engagement opportunities but with the introduction of GS1 standards we can unlock these at product barcode-level making content hyper-relevant and driving exceptionally high dwell-times for brands to build customer loyalty. But GS1 standards will also enable digital product passports, rewards for recycling, authentication and provenance assurances, management of food waste and other supply chain optimisation processes ... these things and more are all unlocked with the use of GS1-compliant codes within connected packaging solutions.

**How do you envision the integration of digital watermarking with other emerging technologies, such as AI and blockchain, in the realm of connected packaging?**

Polytag has a patented innovation (granted in the UK in October 2023 and in the USA in March 2024) for the use of fluorescent ink tags, detected in recycling centres, for the purposes of reporting on EPR. This patent and our innovative solution to detect single-use recyclable plastic in recycling centres is driving significant programmes of work in the UK and across Europe. The use of GS1 standard 2D data matrix to create the fluorescent tags offers the circular economy an opportunity to flourish – no tech lock-in and low-cost, easy-to-apply fluorescent tags will step-change the future of recycling of plastic across the world because all stakeholders in the value chain can interact with the tag to collect data (at barcode level) and act on the tag to enhance sortation capabilities. The Polytag invisible fluorescent tag solution can be deployed anywhere in the world and does not rely on the compilation of huge, labour-intensive AI image-files or carbon-intensive blockchain solutions.

**What are some of the most exciting developments in digital watermarking technology that you believe will impact the future of packaging?**

Polytag's invisible fluorescent tag solution is a zero-disruption addition to standard manufacturing processes for packaging; simply add an extra colour ink to the standard printing process to create GS1 open-standard 2D data matrix containing the barcode number of the product. Suitable for use on rigid plastic bottle labels, in-mould tubs, flexible plastics, tetrapak and more... these tags unlock never-before-seen data about where when and how much packaging is ACTUALLY getting recycled, and what gets measured gets managed. If brands are serious about genuinely wanting to know how successfully they are recycling material and whether their consumers are recycling packaging at home or on the go then these tags will be a key part of any meaningful ESG strategy. In addition, with the development of plastic packaging tax, packaging EPR, digital Deposit Return Schemes, Digital Waste Tracking and PPWR in Europe... barcode level data about recycling rates will be key to meet legislative reporting requirements and fair allocation of fees and funding. Being able to use the same tags to optimise material sortation and recovery is going to be game-changing and Polytag is delighted to be working with some of the largest recycling machine operators in the world to deliver innovation to step-change the future of recycling.

To wrap up our discussion, Alice concluded with this-

"If you believe that legislation and strategy concerning single-use packaging are going to require increasing amounts of granular data to support target setting, benchmarking and reporting, then you would back Connected Packaging solutions (such as Polytag). These solutions unlock never-before-seen data on point of disposal and point of recycling of single-use packaging. Even better if the data can be collected at barcode-level.

Brands need to stop guessing and start knowing where their packaging is once they have sold it into the distribution networks. It is no longer acceptable to manufacture millions of single-use plastic bottles and have no idea what happens to them once they have left the factory...

Scope 1,2 & 3 emissions demand traceability, ESG strategy and GHG emissions planning demand traceability, governments calculating EPR modulated fees demand traceability, brands wanting to source their own rPET to offset plastic packaging tax demand traceability, heck... guess what else – consumers are sick of greenwashing and they are demanding traceability!
All roads lead to more data and more transparency.
Connected Packaging isn't just a marketing channel... it's business critical."


**Technology Summary**

The technologies behind Connected Packaging—QR codes, NFC, Bluetooth beacons, RFID, AR, and digital watermarking—each offer unique capabilities and benefits. They transform traditional packaging into a dynamic, interactive experience, enhancing consumer engagement, improving supply chain management, and providing valuable data insights. As these technologies continue to evolve, the potential for Connected Packaging will only grow, offering even more innovative ways for brands to connect with consumers and stay ahead in a competitive market.

In summary:

- QR codes are the most accessible, not requiring any specific app
- NFC is also highly accessible for users with compatible devices, not requiring a specific app
- Watermarks often require a specific app, making them less immediately accessible
- Beacon technology typically requires a specific app and active Bluetooth, making it the least accessible of these options

| Aspect | QR Codes | Beacon | NFC | DigiMarc Watermarking |
|---|---|---|---|---|
| Campaign Size | Large scale | Medium scale | Niche marketing campaigns that target smaller customers | Medium scale |
| Platform | Web App or native App | Native App | Web App or Native App | Native App |
| Customization | Can be aligned with branding guidelines of a business | Difficult | Restricted | Difficult |
| Consumer Awareness | High | Low | Moderate | Low |
| Usability | • Anyone<br>• Scan with phone camera<br>• Can work up to distance of 1m | • Needs a set up<br>• Relies on bluetooth<br>• Beacons require baterry/power<br>• Works over longer distances up to 50m | • Tap with NFC – enabled device<br>• Relies on shortwave radio frequency<br>• Does not require baterry power<br>• Works over short distances 2–4cm | • Implementation must be made with their special paint or package which then takes longer to implement |
| Common Use | Linked to almost every marketing asset or lead magnet | Most used for networking and tracking | Most frequently used for payments | BTB for recycling |
| Accessibility | • Can be transmitted digitally<br>• Far range<br>• Occasional lighting issues | • Location based<br>• Must be nearby<br>• No lighting issues | • Location based<br>• Must be at close range<br>• No lighting issues | • Location based<br>• Must be at close range<br>• Occasional lighting issues |
| Costs | • Cost to print QR codes<br>• Web app development cheaper than Native App | • £50 per beacon + set up costs<br>• Native App development cost higher than web App | • £0.50 per tag + set up costs<br>• Native App development cost higher than web App | • Re printing for whole package to be set up plus development of App |

# Chapter 3: The Business Case for Connected Packaging

Connected Packaging represents a transformative opportunity for brands to drive value across multiple facets of their businesses. By integrating digital experiences and data capture directly into product packaging, companies can unlock powerful new capabilities in areas like marketing, supply chain, sustainability, regulatory compliance, and inclusivity.

**Marketing and Consumer Engagement**

Enhanced Customer Experiences and Brand Loyalty

A primary benefit of Connected Packaging is fostering deeper engagement through interactive experiences. The Tetra Pak and Emmi GoodDay campaign showcased how a simple QR code can transform packaging into an engaging channel for instantly rewarding customers and telling brand stories. This campaign saw over 218,000 unique engagements averaging over 2 minutes, demonstrating impressive participation. The brand also was able to collect key information on their consumers and their habits allowing the brand to reposition themselves based on the information gathered.

According to **Appetite Creative's 2024 Connected Packaging Survey**, 30.2% of respondents cited "direct interactions with customers" as a key goal. By enabling experiences like games, exclusive content and product storytelling, Connected Packaging elevates the customer's brand interaction and perception of innovation. The GoodDay case highlights how "consumers appreciate [the] efforts to use innovative technology for rewarding loyalty over time."

This strengthened connection can drive brand loyalty and advocacy. Connected products also allow gathering customer data insights to personalise experiences based on preferences. **32.7%** of surveyed businesses aim to "inform product and marketing decisions" using Connected Packaging data.

**80.4%** think that Connected Packaging will be increasingly important to the packaging industry in the next 12 months and beyond.

**Reasons for the rising importance:**

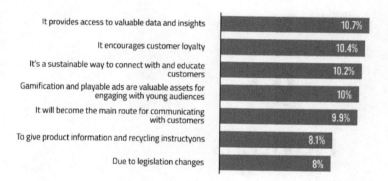

| | |
|---|---|
| It provides access to valuable data and insights | 10.7% |
| It encourages customer loyalty | 10.4% |
| It's a sustainable way to connect with and educate customers | 10.2% |
| Gamification and playable ads are valuable assets for engaging with young audiences | 10% |
| It will become the main route for communicating with customers | 9.9% |
| To give product information and recycling instructyons | 8.1% |
| Due to legislation changes | 8% |

**Inclusivity and Accessibility**

Beyond sustainability, Connected Packaging unlocks opportunities to make product information and brand experiences more inclusive and accessible for people with disabilities or other needs.

For individuals with vision impairment, QR codes that translate to audio product details, instructions and ingredients allow more independence when shopping and using items. This audio capability also benefits those with learning disabilities. For individuals with vision impairment or blindness, Connected Packaging enables independence when shopping and using products. QR codes that audibly relay product details, usage instructions and ingredients via text-to-speech remove barriers.

For people with food allergies or dietary restrictions, Connected Packaging provides easy access to comprehensive, updated details on nutritional information and potential allergens, reducing health risks.

The ability to customise font sizes and toggle between visual and audio information modes makes packaging experiences more accessible overall. This supports regulatory compliance with accessibility standards in different markets.

**NaviLens:**

Developed by the Spanish company NaviLens, the innovative technology allows smartphone cameras to detect unique coded labels from up to 3 metres away when pointed at product packaging. NaviLens even has a sound system so you can find a product easily to pick it up.
Once located and prompted, the phone can then read out all relevant information in an audio format tailored for blind and low-vision users.

Previously deployed in transport networks across Barcelona, Madrid and Murcia to assist the visually impaired, who cannot be autonomous outside.

This technology was first applied to packaging in 2021 with **Coca-Cola UK** was the first beverage brand to pilot NaviLens technology for visually impaired across 24x330ml and 30x330ml packs of its Christmas can multipacks. These codes could be effortlessly scanned from distances of up to four metres, offering valuable assistance to blind and partially sighted consumers in navigating their beverage choices with ease.

Additionally in 2022, in the UK market for food & beverages NaviLens launches Kellogg's accessibility initiative. Partnered with the Royal National Institute of Blind People (RNIB) they launched first-of-its-kind accessible packaging across their entire product range. This landmark initiative leverages cutting-edge NaviLens technology to empower blind and partially sighted consumers to independently access vital product details like ingredients, allergens and recycling information.

**The Accessibility Challenge**

A staggering 9 out of 10 blind and partially sighted individuals find food packaging labelling difficult or impossible to read, according to research by RNIB. This lack of accessibility presents a major barrier, preventing the visually impaired from making confident, well-informed purchasing decisions unaided.

## How It Works

The process is simple - users merely need to download the free NaviLensGO app and point their smartphone towards the desired product on store

shelves. With no need for precise focusing, the codes can be scanned from up to 3 metres away with a wide 160° angle view. The codes as you can see in the image on the left are more colourful than QR codes and actually work a lot faster.

Within just 1/30th of a second, the app detects the unique packaging marker and reads out the complete list of ingredients, allergen information, usage instructions and recycling guidance in a clear audio format. This allows visually impaired shoppers to make fully educated selections independently.

For those with literary, cognitive or learning difficulties affecting reading abilities, having packaging content read aloud offers equally vital accommodation.

## Tackling Food Allergies & Dietary Needs

The widespread prevalence of food allergies and specific dietary requirements like veganism, vegetarianism, kosher or halal makes clear product labelling a necessity rather than a luxury. In Europe alone, over 17 million people suffer from food allergies, including 3.5 million children under 25.

In Spain, a whopping 2 million individuals are impacted, making up 8% of children under 14 and 2-3% of adults. Undeclared allergens and insufficient package information pose serious health risks.

Through its "NaviLens Filtered Ingredients" augmented reality experience, Kellogg's empowers users to toggle filters for food allergens, vegetarian, vegan, halal and kosher preferences. This functionality provides essential transparency and control, allowing the visually impaired and those with dietary restrictions to identify safe, compliant products easily.

The affordable solution enhances regulatory compliance while promoting Kellogg's brand values of inclusivity and consumer empowerment.

**Rolling Out Across Europe**

Spearheading accessible packaging, Kellogg's has already implemented NaviLens codes across all Pringles and Kellogg's products sold in 35 European countries through their Kellanova branch.

This pioneering move earned the "Best In Class" recognition for Inclusive Design at the prestigious PAC Global Leadership Awards in New York.

**"At Kellanova, we are committed to developing inclusive packaging that provides equal opportunities for all. We were the first major CPG company to adopt NaviLens technology, making our products more accessible for the blind and visually impaired since 2022,"** affirmed **Pete Matthews, Design & Brand Operations Director at Kellanova Europe.**

**The Way Forward**

Javier Pita, CEO and Founder of NaviLens, highlighted, **"We've been working alongside Kellanova to make this world more inclusive and accessible**

**through our packaging codes. This enhanced filtered ingredients feature continues our mission of building a society that empowers everyone."**

As societal awareness increases, the demand for accessibility and accommodation will only intensify across consumer markets. With its NaviLens partnership, Kellogg's has taken a pioneering step towards a future where barriers to inclusivity are systematically eliminated through innovative technologies.

By setting an exemplary industry standard for accessible packaging, Kellogg's is paving the way for a more equitable and empowering experience for all consumers, regardless of ability. This trailblazing move encapsulates the brand's steadfast commitment to diversity, inclusivity and helping make the world a little bit better for everyone.

How have the Navilens codes have improvements on the standard QR code?

**LONG DISTANCE**
Capable of reading the labels from long distances, depending on the size of the marker.

**NO FOCUS**
No need for focusing, which is essential for people with visual impairments.

**MOVEMENT**
Navilens algorithm detects the tags when the user is walking or in motion while the cell phone is pointed up.

**PRECISE DISTANCE AND ORIENTATION**
Navilens accurately detects the distance between the user and the tags. In addition, NaviLens provides the relative angle of the user with respect to the tag.

**MULTIPLE READING**

It detects multiple tags simultaneously, efficiently communicating them to the user

Cases like NaviLens demonstrate accessible packaging in action. Their mobile app allows blind users to simply scan product codes to have all packaging information read out loud clearly. This audio capability empowers users to confidently identify, learn about and properly use items without assistance.

Such audio functionality also benefits those with learning disabilities, literacy challenges or cognitive impairments that impact reading abilities. Having packaging content spoken out equitably meets their needs.

**Food Allergies and Dietary Restrictions**

For people with food allergies, dietary restrictions or relevant medical conditions, Connected Packaging provides easy access to comprehensive, updated details on nutritional information, potential allergens/triggers and safe handling instructions.
This transparency reduces health risks and anxiety around unknowingly consuming problematic ingredients. Digitally connected products ensure consumers always have the latest accurate data to make informed, safe decisions.

**Customisable Experiences**

Connected Packaging also allows customising how product experiences are delivered based on individual requirements. Users can toggle between visual and audio/tactile modes, increase font sizes, adjust colour contrasts and more.

This flexibility ensures brand messaging and packaging information is conveyed in an accessible, impactful way across a wide range of abilities. It supports regulatory compliance with accessibility standards across different markets.

The NaviLens platform exemplifies this customisability, offering separate app experiences tailored for sighted, low-vision or blind users to engage with packaging and spaces in their preferred way.
By making packaging interactions more equitable, connected solutions like NaviLens foster inclusivity and independence for people too often excluded from accessible product experiences. This aligns with 26.7% of surveyed businesses citing "educate customers/share information" as a key goal for Connected Packaging initiatives.

From accommodating disabilities to dietary needs, Connected Packaging stands to revolutionise how product information and brand stories are delivered to drive more inclusive, empathetic audience engagement. This accessibility empowers underserved segments while helping brands comply with standards and build reputation as innovators and corporate leaders in inclusivity.

**Supply Chain Optimization**

In addition to enhancing marketing and consumer engagement, Connected Packaging unlocks powerful capabilities for optimising operations and supply chain management. By integrating unique digital identities and data capture into individual product units, brands gain unprecedented visibility and traceability throughout the supply chain.

## Item-Level Traceability

Each connected product is essentially a digitised, serialised asset that can be tracked in real-time as it moves through distribution channels, warehouses, retail chains and into the hands of consumers. This granular track-and-trace functionality prevents inventory divergences and losses from counterfeit, grey market or stolen goods.

Brands can authenticate individual units at any point in the supply chain by scanning the Connected Packaging's digital trigger like a QR code. This enables robust anti-counterfeiting measures and simplifies processes like validating warranties, returns and repairs by accessing the product's digital history and records.

The data insights captured from Connected Packaging allow brands to optimise inventory levels and distribution based on factual demand rather than forecasts and estimates. By understanding the flow of products across sales channels and locations in real-time, businesses can reduce oversupply or stockout incidents.

This visibility helps minimise working capital tied up in unsold, expired or slow-moving inventory that may ultimately be written off. It allows keeping tighter inventory buffers and making informed decisions about production, distribution, merchandising and promotions based on accurate sell-through data.

Additionally, Connected Packaging data provides crucial forward visibility into where individual batches and product lots are being consumed or stocked. This intelligence enables targeted, low-cost safety recalls by identifying and quarantining only the specific impacted products rather than entire shipment or distribution waves.

Grocery Chain Example Major grocery retailers like Walmart and Albertsons have been implementing Connected Packaging solutions to improve their fresh food supply chains. By applying QR codes to crates and packaged produce, they can track those items from the farm or supplier, through distribution, to individual store shelves.

This traceability allows monitoring product quality and freshness based on supply chain time/temps. It helps identify issues like delays or temperature violations that could impact safety or shelf life. The data also optimises ordering and inventory management to reduce oversupply, markdowns and shrink of perishable goods.

According to Albertsons, their connected supply chain reduced food waste by 92% compared to non-traced inventory.

Pharmaceutical Traceability in the pharmaceutical industry serialised Connected Packaging via 2D barcodes and RFID tags enables tracking of drugs from the production line through the entire distribution channel to the final dispenser.

This comprehensive traceability creates a "Pedigree" that records each hand-off and condition change throughout the supply cycle. It helps identify counterfeiting, diversion or tampering issues to ensure patient safety.

Major pharma companies like Eli Lilly and Purdue Pharma have incorporated this level of Connected Packaging specifically to comply with regulatory track-and-trace requirements and prevent counterfeit drugs from entering the legitimate supply chain.

These examples showcase how industries like food/grocery and pharmaceuticals are leveraging Connected Packaging's traceability to optimise inventory management based on real-time data, while also ensuring product quality, safety and anti-counterfeiting measures throughout distribution.

Overall, Connected Packaging empowers brands to exert much tighter control over their products and inventory as digitised assets. The traceability and data insights it provides allow minimising losses, maximising inventory efficiency, and ultimately driving higher profitability through leaner, more agile supply chain operations.

## Authentication

In today's global marketplace, ensuring the authenticity of products has become an increasingly daunting challenge for brands across various industries. The proliferation of counterfeit goods and grey market activities has not only undermined consumer trust but has also posed significant risks to brand reputation and revenue streams. According to recent estimates, global counterfeiting has ballooned into a staggering $3 trillion issue, highlighting the urgent need for robust authentication solutions.

Moreover, regulatory bodies are tightening compliance obligations, requiring brands to demonstrate sustainability, verifiable recycling practices, and comprehensive lifecycle traceability. These initiatives, often centred around digital product passports, further underscore the necessity for secure and transparent product identification methods.

As consumer expectations shift towards connected experiences, brands are compelled to adopt technologies that not only safeguard against counterfeit threats but also engage consumers on a deeper level. However, existing solutions have often fallen short, either due to security vulnerabilities, high costs, or limited consumer interaction capabilities.

According to the AIPIA Smart Packaging- State of The industry report. A survey of 1,500 consumers across Italy, China, France, UK and US found that 87% answered that it is important or extremely important to be able to verify the authenticity of a product.

The company Certilogo has seen 100% annual growth, serving more than 80 of the world's top fashion brands with its product authentication platform.

Addressing these multifaceted challenges demands innovative approaches in connected packaging technology. This ensures that consumers receive genuine products while maintaining brand integrity and trust.

Two companies I'd like to mention in this space particularly are - Lava and Scantrust.

# scantrust:

**Scantrust** began in 2014 as a pioneer of anti-counterfeiting technology for QR codes. Over the past decade, they have expanded into providing a full suite of cloud-based connected packaging solutions across diverse industries like industrial goods, consumer packaged goods, wine & beverage, and lubricants. To date, Scantrust's secure packaging solutions have been deployed on over 1 billion products in 185 countries worldwide.

Their mission is **"to help companies build direct customer connections, combat counterfeiting, and increase supply chain transparency through connected packaging."**

**Secure QR Code Technology**

At the core of Scantrust's offerings is their patented secure QR code technology, which enhances standard QR codes with powerful anti-counterfeiting capabilities. Any existing QR code can be "upgraded" by Scantrust to become a secure gateway for product information and authentication.

**How It Works:**

- A proprietary secure graphic pattern is printed in the centre of the QR code
- Scantrust's scanning technology can detect if a QR code is an original or a copied counterfeit version
- This allows instant product authentication simply by scanning the secure QR code with a smartphone camera

Unlike holograms or NFC tags, Scantrust's secure QR codes provide a highly scalable and cost-effective anti-counterfeiting solution that works with existing printers and standard QR codes.

**Secure QR Code Implementation**

1. **Code Integration**

   Scantrust provides flexible options for integrating their secure QR codes into a brand's printing process. Codes can either be downloaded for use, or Scantrust can directly integrate the codes with a company's existing label printing equipment and workflows.

2. **Equipment Calibration & Code Activation**

   For each printing environment, Scantrust rigorously tests and calibrates the printing of the secure QR codes on the specific equipment to be used. The secure QR codes must go through an activation process before they can be used. Only activated secure QR codes printed through this calibrated setup can be successfully authenticated by end-users.

3. **Authentication by Inspectors or Consumers**

With secure QR codes applied to product packaging, authentication can then be performed by professional inspectors, brand personnel, or even end consumers. Using a standard smartphone camera, they simply scan the secure QR code.

4. **Counterfeit Detection & Alerts**

Scantrust's patented technology can distinguish authenticated secure QR codes from counterfeits or copies. When an in-market or inspector scan detects a counterfeit, the brand is promptly alerted with notification and data on the incident. Brands also receive alerts if a product is scanned without the expected secure QR code present.

5. **Traceability Data & Response**

In addition to counterfeit alerts, Scantrust provides brands with full traceability data and historical records on all secure QR code scans and authentication events. This intelligence allows them to pinpoint sources of counterfeiting and take targeted action to address threats as they are detected throughout the product lifecycle and supply chain.

By streamlining this secure QR code implementation across their operations, brands can establish a full chain of custody authenticated at every step from manufacturing to the end consumer. Scantrust's solution provides an efficient way to combat counterfeiting, increase supply chain transparency, and enable on-demand product authentication and traceability.

Scantrust are also providing QR codes to create digital wine labels to satisfy new E.U. rules, Automatically translated to all E.U. languages. Labels are automatically translated into 24 official EU languages, with the right language shown to customers depending on their smartphone language.

By deploying Secure QR codes, brands can fight counterfeiting, build direct customer connections, provide product transparency, and enable on-demand product authentication and traceability throughout the supply chain.

Authentication of Things™

**Laava** - The company was founded in 2017 based on cybersecurity principles and R&D from scientific institutions worldwide. Laava currently safeguards millions of products globally through partnerships spanning consumer goods, food/beverage, and automotive.

Laava is a technology company focused on product authentication and consumer engagement, instead of QR codes they are using their patented Smart Fingerprint® digital identity technology. Each Smart Fingerprint® provides a unique digital ID that can be scanned by smartphones to verify a product's authenticity in real-time.

Laava's solutions combine overt and covert product identification methods integrated with their digital experience platform, the Laava Product Cloud. This allows brands to protect against counterfeiting, enhance traceability for regulatory compliance, and facilitate consumer engagement.

I had the pleasure of a short interview with **Gavin Gerr, co-founder** of **Lavva**, and I asked him a couple of questions.

**What inspired you to create this platform, and what gap in the market did you aim to fill?**

My early career was focused on technology transformations in the supply chain, and then later on CRM tech for sales & marketing effectiveness. I had always loved these two diverse business functions, but the technology business I was fortunate to become a co-founder of - Laava.id - brought these two things together for me, so it felt like a logical step.

But it was Laava's focus on *authentication* - protecting people and brands from the scourge of counterfeits (which is a deadly serious - and growing -

global problem) - and Laava's support for all 3 of these three use cases and needs via a next generation connected packaging tech - that really lit my fire and drove me to focus on building the business full-time.

6 years later, I'm still with Laava, and am incredibly privileged to lead a world-class team located in the USA, Canada, Europe, Australia and Brazil - who are as passionate about these things - as well as caring for our customers and partners - as I am!

**Can you share some success stories where connected packaging significantly improved brand authenticity and consumer trust?**

The story that always comes to mind for me is one of Laava's first - protecting some of the world's most precious premium foods in China. In many cultures, cherries and other premium fruits are incredibly highly regarded. They are given as a gift to valued business partners as well as loved ones, and part of what makes cherries special is their very short growing season and unique taste and texture when fresh. In fact, the season is often only 6 weeks long, and in places like Tasmania in Australia's far South, they grow slowly in relatively small volumes - and as such are crispy and big - like little apples!

 As a brand new start-up, Laava was very fortunate to be selected to help one of the world's leading cherry brands - Reid Fruits protect their premium export cherries from counterfeits in China, India, Vietnam, UK and other global markets. People often don't believe me when I tell them that Reid Fruits' iconic 2kg gold export grade cherries are air-freighted - going from Tasmania tree to Shanghai table - in only 3 days, and commanding a premium of up to US$200 per 2kg box! When China's President visited Reid Fruits in Tasmania in 2014 (an indication of how seriously China values this product) counterfeiters took note, and started selling look-alike Reid boxes, filled with inferior grade cherries. This not only swindled unsuspecting consumers, it robbed Reid and their official importers of millions of dollars in revenue - and put the brand and consumers at risk of serious health risks (or worse) and brand damage.

It was at this point that Reid Fruits started a years-long battle with counterfeiters - which included major upgrades to embedded security features in packaging, labelling and finally - deployment of QR codes in 2018. All of these measures were copied by counterfeiters, including the QR code authentication system - which was 'spoofed'. Counterfeiters copied Reid Fruit's website and 'authentication' landing pages into a similar sounding domain, and then created their own QR codes which bypassed the real thing to land at the fake authentication landing pages. This is another fact people often think I'm making up, but it shows just how ingenious and determined counterfeiters can be when there's money to be made.

Anyway, it was after the 'spoofed' QR codes issue in 2018 that Reid searched for a next-generation solution, and Laava was selected. I will certainly never forget watching Laava's computer vision technology and GPS tracking system displaying counterfeiters attempting to copy and sell fake boxes of Reid cherries with lookalike Laava Smart Fingerprint labels - and being shut down in real time. This was our first major pilot, but it was also Reid Fruits full annual production - and they were counting on our tech to work. After the previous year's issues, it was 'do or die' for Reid - and frankly for Laava!

Fortunately for us both, the Laava tech worked, and I'm honoured to say that 5 years later, we are still working together. Beyond authentication, Laava, Reid and our China marketing-tech partners Roolife Group - have also rolled out a number of bold on-product consumer engagement, digital storytelling and promotional campaigns, leveraging Chinese social commerce platforms like Little Red Book - with special offers, competitions and pop-up experiences - powered by Laava's secure connected packaging technology. Every year we continue to evolve the consumer experience with new 'surprise-and-delight' connected packaging elements - and level-up the security side with ever improving authentication and traceability measures - all powered by Laava's Smart Fingerprints and Product Cloud. I can't wait for 2025 !!

## What emerging technologies do you believe will further enhance connected packaging and authentication in the next five years?

As we all know, AI is pervading more and more aspects of our lives, and we've all heard the stories of "deep fakes" and other perils that AI technology can enable when used by bad actors. But it can also be used for good. AI and Machine Learning can also be used to trawl the web and monitor for fake products, images, listings and other nefarious activity - and even automatically shut them down in real time.

Laava works with partners who do exactly this, and our long-held belief that "it takes a village" means that we partner very effectively with online monitoring and brand protection specialists, as well as other advanced technology providers - to deploy layered solutions that protect consumers and brands regardless of location or channel. We find that when we collaborate and integrate, we're "better together" - and we can leverage our partners strengths to not only deliver greater active protection, but also deliver truly incredible insights - from consumer purchasing behaviours to web-enabled traceability and inventory control from farm to fork, powered by our partner Pentalym - even tracking the temperature, humidity and vibration in transit, as our partners at Escavox deliver! And we can integrate and serve up an integrated consumer-centric view of all of this via the Laava Digital Experience Builder.

And on the consumers engagement side, we are fortunate to have partners like Appetite Creative - who specialise in delivering world-leading rewards, gamification and digital asset experiences for consumers - which can be integrated directly with Laava's secure smart labels and packaging - as well as many other marketing technology, printing and packaging partners - who collectively help us deliver incredible connected packaging experiences that add significantly to brand value, while delighting consumers.  Not a week goes by at Laava when we aren't evaluating and building new technology features for our customers - not just our own, but through our growing partner ecosystem - and it's fascinating seeing where this can take us all!

From their success in protecting premium products like Reid Fruits cherries to their innovative use of AI and partnerships with other technology leaders, Laava is driving significant advancements in the field. The company's commitment to combining cutting-edge technology with practical business solutions demonstrates the immense potential of smart packaging in combating counterfeiting, enhancing traceability, and creating meaningful consumer experiences.

Connected Packaging technology will continue to shape the landscape of product authentication and connected packaging, offering brands powerful tools to build trust, ensure authenticity, and engage with consumers in increasingly sophisticated ways.

Let's move to another case study within Authentication, as we do so it may be a surprise to learn that the industry estimates suggest that approximately 20% of wine sold worldwide may be counterfeit. The problem is particularly prevalent in certain markets. For example, it's estimated that up to 50% of the wine sold in China could be fake, especially for high-end imported wines.

Rare and expensive wines are more likely to be counterfeited. Some experts believe that for certain premium wines, like rare vintages of Bordeaux or Burgundy, the percentage of fakes could be even higher.

## Case Study

Tamburlaine Organic Wines deployed 1 million Laava Smart Fingerprint codes across their wine bottles and ranges in 2021. The Smart Fingerprints acted as a secure gateway for consumers to access exclusive digital content and brand storytelling from Tamburlaine.

**Objectives**:

- Provide proof of product authenticity
- Allow consumers to connect with Tamburlaine's brand story and sustainability values
- On the True Earth Collective range with Jamie Durie, enable consumers to redeem a sustainable investment offer through the Upstreet app
- Ensure the Upstreet offer could only be redeemed once per Smart Fingerprint code

-

**Results:** Over 16% scan rate of the Smart Fingerprint codes (one of Laava's highest)

- Over 80% conversion rate of scans redeeming the Upstreet investment offer
- Enabled tailored customer experiences for each wine variety

The project allowed Tamburlaine to authentically connect consumers to their brand story, sustainability initiatives, and provide proof of product authenticity - and connected to a reward program as well.

## Sustainability and Regulatory Compliance

As environmental standards and regulations evolve, Connected Packaging enables more sustainable product lifecycles and compliance. Digital product passports can capture details like embodied carbon footprints, materials data and environmental impacts through the supply chain.

This transparency allows verifying products meet evolving green standards and labelling laws across markets. Connected Packaging data provides proof of sustainable sourcing and ethical manufacturing for conscious consumers. The 2024 survey found 90.7% of participants agreed it could elevate their sustainability credentials.

For end consumers, QR codes can provide recycling instructions, depot locations and proper disposal information by product to drive more sustainable behaviour. This aligns with the 19.3% of surveyed businesses aiming to show "Connected Packaging is a sustainable way to engage customers."

The packaging industry is witnessing a significant shift towards sustainability and digital integration, with connected packaging emerging as a powerful tool to address both marketing needs and regulatory requirements. This evolution is particularly evident in the rise of Deposit Return Schemes (DRS) across Europe and beyond, showcasing how technology can bridge the gap between consumer engagement and environmental responsibility.

Connected packaging, particularly through the use of QR codes and other digital technologies, is playing a crucial role in the implementation of DRS. These systems, mandated by evolving packaging legislation, aim to increase recycling rates and reduce environmental impact. The European Union's Packaging and Packaging Waste Regulation, for instance, sets ambitious targets for the separate collection of single-use plastic bottles and metal beverage containers, with DRS seen as a key method to achieve these goals.

From a marketing perspective, connected packaging in DRS offers brands unique opportunities:

1. **Consumer Engagement**: QR codes on packaging can provide information about the DRS process, encouraging participation and educating consumers about sustainability efforts.
2. **Brand Loyalty**: By facilitating easy returns and refunds, brands can enhance customer experience and build loyalty.
3. **Data Collection:** Connected packaging enables the collection of valuable data on consumer behaviour and recycling patterns, informing future marketing strategies and product development.
4. **Sustainability Messaging:** Brands can use connected packaging to communicate their environmental initiatives directly to consumers, strengthening their eco-friendly image.

The implementation of DRS across various countries demonstrates the growing importance of connected packaging in meeting regulatory requirements:

- Romania launched one of the world's largest centralised DRS in November 2023, utilising digital systems to manage deposits and returns.
- Austria plans to introduce a DRS in January 2025, aiming for high collection rates through digitally-enabled return systems.
- Latvia's two-year-old system has already seen significant increases in collection rates, with high consumer participation.
- Ireland's recent introduction of DRS highlights the need for clear communication, which connected packaging can address.

However, the transition to DRS and connected packaging is not without challenges. Some local authorities and industry players have expressed concerns about implementation costs and potential impacts on existing recycling systems. These concerns underscore the importance of designing connected packaging solutions that are not only compliant with regulations but also cost-effective and user-friendly.

The success of connected packaging in DRS relies heavily on consumer adoption. Surveys indicate generally positive attitudes towards these systems, with many consumers expressing willingness to participate when they understand the environmental benefits. This presents an opportunity for brands to use connected packaging as an educational tool, further enhancing its marketing potential.

Looking ahead, connected packaging is set to play an increasingly vital role in meeting sustainability targets and regulatory requirements. As legislation like the EU's Packaging and Packaging Waste Regulation continues to evolve, brands that effectively integrate connected packaging into their DRS strategies will be well-positioned to meet compliance standards while also leveraging these systems for marketing and consumer engagement.

In conclusion, Connected Packaging, when applied to initiatives like DRS, represents a convergence of marketing innovation, sustainability efforts, and regulatory compliance. By embracing these technologies, brands can not only meet legal requirements but also enhance their market position, engage consumers more effectively, and contribute to broader environmental goals.

**Looking Ahead**

The impressive growth trajectory for Connected Packaging is clear from the survey data, which found **81.9%** of respondents already utilising it in 2024, up sharply from just **44% in 2022**. This highlights how crucial the technology has become as a competitive differentiator and necessity for modern brands.

When asked to rate Connected Packaging's importance for their business in 2024 on a scale of 1-10, a striking 76% of respondents answered between 7-10. This reflects heightened expectations that connected experiences will be pivotal for driving objectives and meeting evolving consumer demands in the coming year and beyond.

## HOW IMPORTANT WILL CONNECTED PACKAGING BE TO YOUR BUSINESS IN 2024?

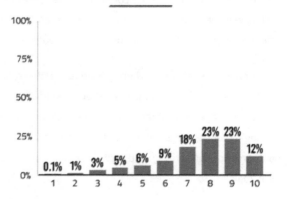

From marketing and consumer connections to operational efficiency, sustainability initiatives and accessible product experiences, implementing Connected Packaging provides brands a holistic solution to create value across their business. As real-world cases like GoodDay's campaign demonstrate, this technology elevates products while tangibly benefitting the brand.

The comprehensive industry data and cases highlighted throughout "Connected Packaging: Bridging the Gap Between Physical and Digital Experiences eBook Appetite Creative" underscore Connected Packaging's revolutionary impact across consumer markets. By exploring the technology's definition, importance, benefits, applications, inclusivity factors and future prospects, this guide provides invaluable insights for any business aiming to capitalise on Connected Packaging's transformative potential.

From our experience, and our Connected Packing Report we see the biggest rise in interest is within the Alcoholic Beverages and CPG categories.

Building connected consumer journeys will be vital to enabling brands to adopt data-led strategies. First-party data is a hot topic for brands, with a huge 80.4% declaring that Connected Packaging will be increasingly important to the packaging industry in the next 12 months and beyond.

Informing users about the product and data collection being the top two reasons why they consider Connected Packaging important.

Brands are using this data for everything from New Product Development to marketing spend optimisation across the funnel.  Bringing together in a real way seamlessly linking connected out-of-home media, product packaging, events, including rewards, exclusive access, and retailer and stockist maps - all anchored by a QR code that allows continuous personalised engagement through repeated scanning. All alongside the connected experience triggered through the QR code on-packs.

Connected packaging represents a powerful tool, arguably the brand's MOST powerful owned media channel. It is their owned media channel, for brands to enhance their relationship with consumers while streamlining operations and promoting sustainability. By leveraging digital loyalty programs, instant win promotions, and personalised content, brands can significantly boost engagement and foster brand loyalty. The authentication capabilities combat counterfeiting, while improved accessibility features like NaviLens ensure inclusivity for all users. Furthermore, connected packaging enables brands to communicate their sustainability initiatives effectively and provide crucial product origin information. As we move forward, the integration of these technologies into packaging strategies will not only improve the customer experience but also provide valuable data insights, enabling brands to make informed decisions and stay competitive in an increasingly digital marketplace.

The business case for connected packaging is clear: it's an innovative solution that bridges the physical and digital worlds, offering benefits that extend far beyond the product itself.

# Chapter 4: Case Studies and Industry Examples

In this next chapter, we embark on a global tour of innovative packaging solutions in the marketing and FMCG (Fast-Moving Consumer Goods) sectors. Our journey showcases the ingenuity and creativity of various companies we've collaborated with at Appetite Creative.

Appetite Creative, the digital experiences studio, connects brands to today's audiences. We specialise in using innovative technology to deliver connected brand experiences that help advertisers better understand audiences, optimise marketing, drive sales, and improve two-way customer communications. We are pioneers in Connected Packaging. For this chapter, I've selected case studies from different regions, each presenting unique challenges and opportunities in the packaging industry. These examples highlight how connected packaging is revolutionising marketing strategies and consumer engagement for FMCG brands worldwide.

From the vibrant markets of the West Indies to the modern cityscapes of Saudi Arabia and Kuwait, through the rich cultural tapestry of European countries like Spain, Portugal, Austria, and Croatia, to the diverse landscapes of Guatemala, The Philippines and South Africa, we present a collection of remarkable case studies that demonstrate the power of creative packaging.

Each case study in this chapter offers a unique glimpse into how cutting-edge technologies and collaborative approaches have addressed specific challenges and unlocked new possibilities in vastly different markets. These stories not only showcase technical innovation but also highlight the cultural nuances and market-specific demands that shape packaging solutions worldwide.

As we explore these diverse examples, readers will gain invaluable insights into:

1. Adapting packaging designs to meet local preferences and regulations
2. Overcoming unique environmental and logistical challenges
3. Incorporating traditional aesthetics with modern functionality
4. Pioneering sustainable solutions in various global contexts
5. Leveraging technology to enhance brand storytelling and consumer engagement

## Emmi's New Flavour Promotion Using Augmented Reality and Smart Packaging – Education about a new flavour

Challenge

Swiss milk processor Emmi, Tetra Pak, and Appetite Creative collaborated on an AR Connected Experience using Smart Packaging. The interactive AR-enabled experience is accessible through Emmi's Tetra Stelo Aseptic 1000 packaging, promoting healthier lifestyles and enhancing brand recognition.

Solution

The first step was to collaborate closely with Emmi and Tetra Pak, understanding their vision and goals. Appetite Creative designed an interactive and visually appealing AR-enabled experience that would be accessed through Emmi's new Tetra Stelo Aseptic 1000 packaging. The sleek packaging design served as a gateway to an augmented reality world, where users could unlock a range of experiences designed to inspire healthier and happier lifestyles.

The AR experience began with users simply scanning the packaging using their mobile phone cameras. Immediately, an enchanting AR animation enveloped the packaging, introducing users to a menu of immersive experiences. Alongside the engaging visuals, we incorporated fun facts about the packaging improvements to educate and entertain users.

To make the experience even more captivating, Appetite Creative developed interactive games within the web-based app. One such game, "Move your Body," allowed users to select from three new milk drink options: Barista, High Protein, or Milk Drink. Through this game, users learned about the different drinks while collecting virtual fruit, oats, and other ingredients in a digital cereal bowl. Appetite Creative also created the "Breakfast Ninja" game, where users raced against time to slice various breakfast ingredients. Each game concluded with updated recipe ideas and inspirational quotes, providing users with additional value beyond entertainment.

Furthermore, to incentivise participation and enhance user engagement, Appetite Creative introduced a leaderboard system where users earned points based on their interactions. Weekly winners on the leaderboard had the chance to win exciting prizes, including Apple Watches, yoga mats, and milk frothers. By encouraging users to share their experiences on social media, brand awareness was boosted and their engagement further amplified.


Results

The launch of this AR-Connected Experience proved to be a resounding success for both Emmi and Tetra Pak. The collaboration between Appetite

Creative and Emmi yielded impressive engagement metrics, with users spending an average of just under 2 minutes interacting with the experience and generating over 250k page views. This high level of interaction demonstrated the appeal of the AR games and content across all age groups. The web-based app's real-time tracking capabilities provided Emmi with valuable insights into customer preferences and behaviours, allowing for dynamic adaptation of marketing messages. This agility in messaging helped foster authentic connections with customers. Furthermore, the campaign's integration with social media channels amplified its reach, generating buzz and facilitating widespread sharing. As a result, Emmi experienced significant increases in brand recognition and overall image enhancement, showcasing the power of connected packaging in creating meaningful customer engagement.

Conclusion

The collaboration between Appetite Creative, Emmi, and Tetra Pak serves as a prime example of the successful implementation of augmented reality and Smart Packaging. By seamlessly blending technology, packaging design, and interactive experiences, healthier and happier lifestyles among consumers was inspired. The AR-Connected Experience not only captured the attention of customers but also enabled Emmi to connect with them on a deeper level, fostering brand loyalty and advocacy. This case study highlights the immense potential of AR and smart packaging to revolutionise the way brands engage with their clients.

**Showcasing the KDD beverage range via an engaging connected experience - Back to school campaign moment engagement**

In the wake of the global pandemic, KDD faced the challenge of reconnecting with children and families as schools reopened. To address this, Appetite Creative developed a captivating Connected Experiences campaign for KDD, featuring interactive games and augmented reality (AR) filters. This case study highlights the successful execution of the campaign and its impact on engagement and brand recognition.

## Challenge

After an extended period of school closures, KDD aimed to engage young students and their families by offering an interactive experience centred around their juice and milk drinks. The objective was to develop an appealing game that showcased the KDD beverage range, fostering connections with users of all ages.

## Solution

Appetite Creative devised a multi-level experience that incorporated a 2D racing game, an AR game, and a selection of AR filters. Users accessed the games and filters by scanning a QR code found on KDD products. The initial racing game involved a personalised car representing the user's favourite KDD flavour, requiring players to navigate obstacles and collect boosting ingredients for improved leaderboard rankings.

Upon completing the racing game, users unlocked the AR game titled "What's in my lunchbox?" Leveraging the smartphone's camera, this game presented a three- dimensional space where KDD products and fruit were launched from a lunchbox. Players had to swiftly slice the items using their chosen 3D character, competing against time in three different levels. Additionally, users were encouraged to share their results on social media, increasing their chances of winning prizes.

## Results

Within the first three months since its launch in September, the campaign achieved impressive results. Over 100,000 scans were recorded, with the games played more than 191,000 times. Users spent an average session duration of 2 minutes and 39 seconds, showcasing the engaging nature of the experience and resulting in a low bounce rate of 1.09%.

Furthermore, more than 10k users submitted their data to appear on the leaderboard, providing valuable insights for KDD. The campaign's call-to-action for sharing on social media proved successful, with over 2,600 shares across platforms such as WhatsApp, Twitter, and Facebook.

Conclusion

The collaboration between Appetite Creative and KDD demonstrated the power of Connected Experiences to engage and reconnect with audiences. By leveraging interactive games and AR filters, KDD successfully captured the attention of young students and their families, fostering brand loyalty and generating valuable user data. The campaign's impressive performance in terms of scans, game plays, and social media shares highlights the effectiveness of creative and immersive experiences in driving brand engagement and recognition.

# Woodlands Dairy - Educating consumers about the importance of sustainability through a connected experience

This case study explores the successful sustainability campaign undertaken by Woodlands Dairy in collaboration with Tetra Pak and Appetite Creative. The study highlights the challenges faced in effectively communicating sustainability initiatives, the strategic solutions implemented, and the remarkable results achieved in engaging the target audience, increasing participation, and promoting Woodlands Dairy as a brand dedicated to sustainability within the dairy industry.

## Challenge

Woodlands Dairy faced the challenge of effectively communicating its sustainability initiatives and educating consumers about the importance of sustainability in the dairy industry. The goal was to engage a diverse audience, with a specific focus on mothers and children, by capturing their attention, encouraging participation, and positioning Woodlands Dairy as a brand that prioritises sustainability. Additionally, the campaign aimed to provide an interactive and educational experience that would resonate with the target audience.

## Solution

To overcome these challenges, Woodlands Dairy partnered with Tetra Pak and enlisted the expertise of Appetite Creative to create an interactive experience that would educate and engage consumers. Through the simple act of scanning a QR code on Tetra Pak cartons, consumers were able to embark on an interactive journey. This experience included a quiz with short and engaging questions designed to educate consumers about sustainability and offer insights into Woodlands Dairy's green initiatives. To boost engagement, Woodlands Dairy incentivised participation by offering 13,500R shopping vouchers as prizes in a weekly draw. Sharing the winners on social media channels generated additional excitement and raised awareness about Woodlands Dairy's sustainability efforts.

## Results

Since the campaign's launch in March, there has been a remarkable surge in growth, which can be attributed to the strategic promotion and weekly announcement of winners on social media. This approach significantly contributed to increased engagement and participation.

The campaign successfully attracted a predominantly female audience, with women comprising 78% of participants. This aligns with the campaign's focus on mothers and highlights the effectiveness of targeting this demographic.

The desired age demographic of 25-36 was effectively reached, as participants within this age group formed the largest proportion of the campaign's audience.

The campaign received substantial traffic from Facebook, indicating that sharing 31 winners on this social media platform yielded excellent results. This strategy successfully attracted visitors and increased visibility for the campaign.

The campaign achieved a below-average bounce rate of only 18%, indicating that the interactive experience successfully captured users' attention and encouraged further engagement. The average user engagement time of 2 minutes and 14 seconds suggests that participants actively interacted with the content, spending a significant amount of time learning about Woodlands Dairy's sustainability initiatives. Most importantly, there was a 30% increase in sales.

## Conclusion

The collaboration between Tetra Pak, Woodlands Dairy, and Appetite Creative for the sustainability campaign proved highly successful in educating consumers, engaging the target audience, and promoting Woodlands Dairy as a brand committed to sustainability. The interactive experience, accessed through scanning QR codes on Tetra Pak cartons, effectively captured users' attention and encouraged active participation, as demonstrated by the rapid growth, increased engagement, and favourable user engagement metrics. The campaign's strategic use of social media, particularly in sharing winners and raising awareness, further contributed to its achievements. Overall, this campaign successfully communicated Woodlands Dairy's sustainability initiatives, resonated with the target audience, enhanced the brand's reputation as an environmentally conscious leader in the dairy industry, and increased its sales.

## Don Simon from Garcia Carrion-Enhancing sustainability engagement and highlighting new packaging materials and incorporating loyalty program

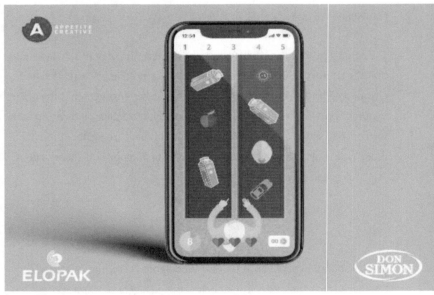

In an effort to prioritise sustainability and engage consumers, Don Simon introduced a new range of Pure-Pak eSense packs with a web app-based Connected Experience. Accessible through QR codes, this innovative packaging aims to educate consumers about its aluminium- free carton, renewable plastic cap, and unbleached natural brown board. This case study explores how Appetite Creative successfully integrated sustainability and interactivity to create an engaging and data-driven campaign.

## Challenge

Don Simon recognised the importance of incorporating sustainability into every aspect of their brand. They sought to educate consumers about their eco- friendly packaging and make recycling both convenient and enjoyable. The challenge was to design a Connected Experience that not only emphasised sustainability but also encouraged consumer participation and provided valuable insights for the brand.

## Solution

Appetite Creative developed a web app-based Connected Experience that transformed Don Simon's packaging into a platform for interactive engagement. Upon scanning the QR code, consumers were immersed in a range of sustainability- themed games and educational content.

The interactive games included activities such as creating packaging from sustainable materials, developing products from plants, and learning about carton recycling. These experiences aimed to educate and entertain consumers while emphasising the brand's commitment to sustainability.

Furthermore, the web app employed real-time tracking capabilities, capturing valuable data on consumer behaviour and preferences. This data encompassed buying habits, product preferences, average engagement time, location, scan rate, number of visitors, return visitors, and GDPR-compliant personal data. By collecting this information, Don Simon gained insights into consumer engagement, enabling them to refine marketing strategies and enhance their sustainability initiatives.

Jenny Stanley, managing director at Appetite Creative, emphasised the campaign's focus on sustainability and consumer involvement. The ambassador competition, offered through the Connected Experience, not only rewarded consumers with early access to new products and brand updates but also provided an opportunity for passionate consumers to become engaged influencers for the brand.

Results

The Don Simon Connected Experience campaign proved to be a resounding success, both in terms of consumer engagement and data collection. The interactive games and educational content captivated consumers, driving increased awareness of the brand's sustainable packaging. The real-time tracking capabilities provided Don Simon with valuable insights into consumer behaviours and preferences, enabling them to tailor their marketing strategies effectively. The twelve month campaign had an average engagement time of over 3 minutes.

By combining sustainability messaging with gamified experiences, Don Simon encouraged consumers to actively participate in recycling efforts. The campaign's ambassador competition further amplified consumer involvement and fostered a community of passionate brand advocates. It also challenged consumer behaviour as the discounts offered were for the brands online platform.

Conclusion

The collaboration between Don Simon and Appetite Creative resulted in a compelling case study on the integration of sustainability and Connected Packaging. By leveraging a web app-based Connected Experience accessible via QR codes, Don Simon successfully educated and engaged consumers about their eco-friendly packaging solutions. The interactive games and data-driven insights not only strengthened the brand's commitment to sustainability but also fostered a community of dedicated brand advocates. This case study highlights the power of interactive packaging experiences in driving consumer engagement, increasing brand loyalty, and collecting valuable data for strategic marketing decisions.

## Gulf Union's Engaging and Memorable Back-to-School Experience to increase engagement and CRM data

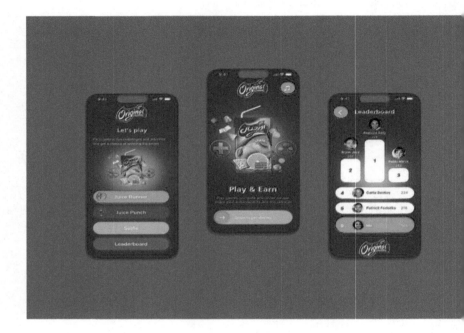

Gulf Union, a leading juice brand, partnered with Appetite Creative, a creative tech studio specialising in Connected Packaging, to launch an innovative Back to School campaign aimed at schoolchildren. The campaign aimed to create an engaging and memorable experience for young consumers, utilising technology to enhance their interaction with Gulf Union's products in Saudi Arabia. This experience comprised two captivating games: "Juice Punch" and "Juice Run." The central objective was to establish how Gulf Union's juices could provide an energy boost to kids as they returned to school, making their start of the school year exciting and invigorating.

## Challenge

The core challenge was to captivate the attention of schoolchildren and create an experience that resonated with them, ensuring that Gulf Union's products were seen as a vital part of their Back to School preparations. The campaign needed to overcome the common marketing hurdles of reaching and engaging a young demographic. Moreover, the challenge was to convey the message that Gulf Union juices could provide the energy and enthusiasm needed for a successful start to the school year.

## Solution

To address these challenges, Gulf Union collaborated with Appetite Creative to devise an interactive and playful experience. The campaign introduced two games, "Juice Punch" and "Juice Run," both designed to entertain and educate. "Juice Punch" engaged players with IQ-based challenges, subtly communicating how the juices could enhance cognitive abilities. "Juice Run" tested players' speed and attention, symbolising the energetic boost Gulf Union's juices offered.

The experience was further enriched with a "Selfies" section, allowing players to adorn themselves with a fruity tiara and capture the moment. A "Leaderboard" feature fostered friendly competition, enabling participants to see their rankings and encouraging repeated engagement.

## Results

Engaging Back to School Experience: The campaign successfully achieved its goal of creating an engaging and exciting Back to School experience. The interactive games resonated with school children, effectively communicating Gulf Union's message of energy and empowerment. The campaign was so successful in engaging user that it was extended from a 3-month campaign to a 12-month-long engagement platform. In some months the average engagement time was over 3 minutes and the rescan rate was 7 times per user.

Enhanced Brand Perception: Gulf Union's collaboration with Appetite Creative elevated the brand's image among its young consumers. The interactive experience associated the brand with fun, vitality, and education, fostering a stronger connection between students and Gulf Union juices.

Educational Engagement: The IQ-focused "Juice Punch" game seamlessly blended entertainment and education. It subtly conveyed the message that Gulf Union's juices could provide cognitive benefits, aligning well with the campaign's goal.

Amplified Digital Interaction: The integration of QR codes with the interactive experience streamlined digital engagement, offering students easy access to the games. This approach not only facilitated participation but also provided Gulf Union with valuable insights into user behaviour.

Conclusion

The Back to School campaign by Gulf Union, in partnership with Appetite Creative, successfully captivated the attention of schoolchildren by integrating fun and interactive games that highlighted the energetic benefits of Gulf Union's juices.

Through the innovative use of technology and engaging content, the campaign not only enhanced brand perception among young consumers but also seamlessly combined entertainment with education, reinforcing Gulf Union's position as a vibrant and essential part of the school experience.

This case study highlights the success of creative, technology-driven marketing strategies in engaging a young audience and fostering brand loyalty.

## Jus de Fruits Caraïbes´s promotion of sustainability, responsible recycling, and supporting the local community

Jus de Fruits Caraïbes, a fruit juice brand based in the French West Indies, partnered with creative technology studio Appetite Creative to launch a smart and interactive Connected Packaging experience. The project aimed to raise awareness about the brand's sustainability credentials and support the local community. The campaign featured Banga, an exotic fruit drinks brand under Schweppes International, and utilised a web app accessed via QR codes on the packaging.

### Challenge

Jus de Fruits Caraïbes faced the challenge of engaging consumers in their sustainability journey while promoting responsible beverage carton recycling. They also wanted to find a meaningful way to give back to the local community and raise awareness about their commitment to positive environmental practices. Furthermore, with the impending European Single Use Plastic Directive, the brand needed to introduce the new tethered caps mandated by the directive in a way that would be interesting and educational for consumers.

## Solution

To address the challenges, the team developed a Connected Packaging experience that combined entertainment, education, and charitable giving. The web app enabled users to play an entertaining fall game where they sliced virtual fruit to create fruit juice. Each participation in the game triggered a small donation to a local children's charity, thus ensuring support for those in need.

The connected experience also included a quiz to educate customers on how to recycle the beverage cartons responsibly and to improve their understanding of the brand's sustainability initiatives. Additionally, the web app explained the environmental benefits of the new tethered caps and how to use them effectively. The fun and educational experience powered by Appetite Creative allowed the brand to introduce the new caps in an engaging way.

## Results

The campaign generated an average engagement time of 2 minutes and 37 seconds, over 20.9k game submissions, with peak daily registration numbers at 172 users. The majority of participants, at 32%, were aged between 18-24 years, followed closely by those aged 25-34, at 26%, and 35-44, at 17%. Showing the campaign's effectiveness in capturing the attention of younger demographics.

Most of the product packaging QR code scans originated from the Banga Multifruits 2L product, generating 48% of total scans. By the end of the campaign, 4.7k customer emails had been collected for marketing purposes.

Three key benefits that emerged from the campaign included:
Positive Brand Perception: Consumers association of brand's innovative use of technology for sustainability and charitable purposes, enhancing its reputation.
Enhanced Sustainability Awareness: The campaign encouraged eco-minded behaviour and responsible recycling practices, aligning with the brand's sustainability goals. By encouraging responsible beverage carton recycling in its users, and fostering sustainability knowledge through its quiz section.
Community Engagement: By making charitable donations for each game participation, the brand demonstrated its commitment to giving back to the community, strengthening its bond with customers. In total the campaign generated a donation of 5,515 Euros to the chosen charity, Association Les P'tits Doudous de Cornouaille.

## Conclusion

By leveraging a smart and interactive Connected Packaging experience, Jus de Fruits Caraïbes not only raised awareness about its sustainability initiatives but also engaged consumers in an entertaining and educational manner. Through charitable donations for each game participation, the campaign demonstrated a commitment to giving back to the community, further enhancing the brand's reputation and strengthening its bond with customers.

Overall, the campaign exemplifies the power of innovative marketing strategies in driving positive social and environmental impact.

**Enhancing customer engagement and loyalty for Goodday drinks with instant win competition**

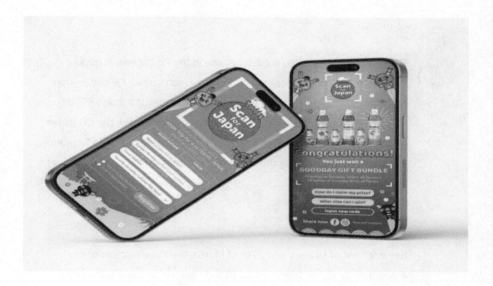

Asahi Beverages Philippines, in collaboration with Universal Robina Corporation and creative technology studio Appetite Creative, embarked on a groundbreaking marketing campaign aimed at enhancing customer engagement and loyalty for its flagship product, Goodday, a cultured milk drink. This case study delves into the details of this innovative connected packaging campaign, highlighting its objectives, strategies, implementation, and outcomes.

Challenge

To increase brand awareness and visibility of Goodday drinks in the Philippines market. To foster direct interaction and engagement with customers through innovative packaging solutions. To incentivise purchases and reward customer loyalty. To collect valuable consumer data for marketing optimisation and better understanding of consumer preferences.

## Solution

The campaign was rolled out nationwide in the Philippines across supermarkets, convenience stores, and sari-sari stores. QR codes were prominently displayed on the packaging of Goodday 80ml and 350ml bottles, ensuring accessibility for consumers. Additionally, the QR codes were made available through Goodday's social media pages on Facebook and Instagram, extending the reach of the campaign to online audiences.

## Results

Between 1st of January and 27th of March, the Total number of scans amounted to 13,3 k; there were 218 k Unique visitors and 8,2k emails collected.

The connected packaging campaign facilitated direct interaction with customers, resulting in increased engagement and brand loyalty.

The innovative campaign garnered widespread attention, effectively boosting brand awareness and visibility in the competitive beverage market.

Real-time data tracking provided valuable insights into consumer behaviour and preferences, enabling Asahi Beverages Philippines to optimise marketing strategies and tailor future campaigns to meet customer needs.

The campaign reinforced Goodday's reputation as a forward-thinking and customer-centric brand, further strengthening its position in the market.

## Conclusion

The Goodday connected packaging campaign exemplifies the power of The Goodday connected packaging campaign exemplifies the power of innovative marketing strategies in driving customer engagement and loyalty. By leveraging connected packaging technology and partnering with experts like Appetite Creative, Asahi Beverages Philippines successfully created a fun and rewarding experience for its customers while gaining valuable insights for future marketing endeavours. This case study underscores the importance of embracing technology and creativity in modern marketing campaigns to stay ahead in an ever-evolving consumer landscape.

# Tetra Pak's Smart Packaging Brings Sustainability to Life

Creative technology studio Appetite Creative has created a new side panel on-pack communication for world-leading food processing and packaging company Tetra Pak across its packaging in Spain and Portugal and mid-Europe including Germany and Austria.

## Challenge

Tetra Pak, a world-leading food processing and packaging company, sought to enhance its on-pack communication to better engage customers and educate them about sustainability. The primary challenge was to create an interactive and educational experience that could be easily accessed by a diverse customer base across Spain, Portugal, and mid-Europe, including Germany and Austria. Tetra Pak wanted to leverage innovative technology to provide valuable insights into consumer behaviour while promoting sustainability.

## Solution

To address this challenge, Appetite Creative, a creative technology studio, developed a new side panel on-pack communication for Tetra Pak. This updated packaging features QR codes that grant users access to a multi-language web app, offering a smart and connected packaging experience. The web app includes a variety of fun and interactive educational games designed to teach users about sustainability.

The Collector Game: Users operate a dump truck to traverse roads, collecting as many Tetra Pak packages as possible while avoiding hazards.
The Memory Game: Players match recycling-themed cards within a set time limit.
The Quiz Game: Tests users' general knowledge about sustainability.
By completing these games, users can win and collect various mission badges. Additionally, the app provides access to Tetra Pak's website, which outlines the company's sustainability initiatives.

The interactive experience was created by Appetite Creative with graphic design by Advertising Design Studio. This collaboration ensured that the experience was both engaging and visually aligned with Tetra Pak's brand identity.

## Results

The connected packaging experience successfully engaged users and provided valuable insights into consumer behaviour. Key outcomes included:

Enhanced Customer Interaction: The interactive games and educational content resulted in increased customer engagement, with users spending an average of three minutes interacting with the app.

Valuable Consumer Data: The web app tracked real-time interactions, including buying habits, product preferences, average engagement time, location, scan rate, number of visitors, return visitors, and social media shares. This data, compliant with GDPR, enabled Tetra Pak to optimise its marketing strategies and better understand consumer behaviour. Increased Awareness of Sustainability: The engaging and educational content raised consumer awareness about sustainability, aligning with Tetra Pak's commitment to environmental responsibility.

Positive Feedback: Both Tetra Pak and the brands who have implemented this across their cartons have, expressed satisfaction with the innovative approach and its effectiveness in educating consumers and enhancing brand loyalty.

The campaign is still running so further results are not ready to be published. However, we are collecting lots of valuable data points in our back end dashboard and we know there are impressive scan engagement times.

## Conclusion

The collaboration between Tetra Pak and Appetite Creative resulted in a groundbreaking connected packaging experience that successfully addressed the initial challenge. By integrating QR codes and a multi-language web app with interactive educational games, Tetra Pak is not only engaging customers but also gathers valuable insights into their behaviour. The campaign, which will run for 12 months, exemplifies how innovative technology can transform packaging into a powerful tool for education and customer engagement, paving the way for more sustainable practices in the FMCG industry. This is an excellent way to communicate sustainability messaging directly to your consumer.

## Lessons Learned

From these any many other case studies and campaigns we have learnt a great many lessons, the key learnings and insights are-

**Incentivisation** drives engagement: Offering prizes significantly increases participation rates. Proper promotion and strategic placement of QR codes are crucial for maximising interaction.

**Multi-channel promotion is essential**: Success relies heavily on a combination of social media, point-of-sale media, and traditional advertising channels like television.

**Technology enhances customer experience:** Interactive elements like games, AR filters, and educational content can significantly boost engagement and brand loyalty.

**Sustainability messaging resonates:** Consumers respond positively to brands that communicate their eco-friendly initiatives through connected packaging.

**Data collection is valuable:** These campaigns provide crucial insights into consumer behaviour, preferences, and engagement patterns.

**Multi-language support expands reach:** Offering content in multiple languages can significantly increase the campaign's accessibility and effectiveness. The cost for this is minimal. Use it.

**Brand perception enhancement:** Creative, technology-driven strategies can positively impact how consumers view the brand, especially among younger audiences.

**Sales impact:** On average there is an increase in sales of 20% - Woodlands Dairy, reported significant sales increases (30%) attributed to connected packaging initiatives.

## Challenges:

Throughout our experience in planning and executing Connected Packaging campaigns, including the case studies we've explored and numerous others, we've identified several recurring challenges.. The most significant challenges we've encountered are:

**Technology adoption:** Ensuring consumers are comfortable with and willing to use QR codes and web apps or cameras, especially in the case of Augmented reality. It will ask for access to your camera will your target audience be ok with that?

**Content relevance:** Creating engaging, interactive content that resonates with the target audience.

**Balancing entertainment and education:** Striking the right balance between fun elements and informative content.

**Technical implementation:** Integrating connected packaging technology seamlessly with existing packaging and production processes. How do we get the QRs or /NFC onto the pack?

**ROI measurement:** Accurately measuring the campaign itself can then allow the brand to measure return on investment for these campaigns, particularly in terms of long-term brand loyalty and sales impact.

**Final Thoughts:**

Connected packaging campaigns continually demonstrate significant potential in driving customer engagement, increasing brand loyalty, and providing valuable consumer insights. When executed well, these initiatives can lead to tangible benefits such as increased sales and enhanced brand perception. The key to success lies in creating a well-rounded strategy that combines innovative technology, engaging content, multi-channel promotion, and a clear value proposition for the consumer.

Crucially, the success of these campaigns often hinges on partnering with experienced agencies or consultants who specialize in connected packaging solutions. Companies like Appetite Creative, or other agencies with a proven track record in this field, bring invaluable expertise to the table. They understand the nuances of designing effectively connected experiences, implementing the right technologies, and measuring campaign success. Their knowledge can be instrumental in navigating potential challenges and maximising the return on investment.

As technology continues to evolve, connected packaging is likely to become an increasingly important tool in the marketing and branding toolkit for consumer goods companies. However, to fully leverage its potential, brands should consider collaborating with expert partners who can guide them through the complexities of this innovative marketing approach and help ensure campaign success.

# Chapter 5: The Consumer Experience

**Interactive Engagement**

Connected packaging transforms traditional packaging into an interactive experience that engages consumers in novel ways. Through technologies like QR codes, NFC tags, and AR experiences, consumers are no longer just passive recipients of product information—they become active participants in a brand's narrative. Connected Packaging is a two-way communication channel.

**How Consumers Interact with Connected Packaging**

1. **Scanning QR Codes:** Consumers can scan QR codes with their smartphones to access a wealth of information, such as product details, usage tips, and promotional content. This instant access to digital content enhances the user experience and provides immediate value.

2. **Near Field Communication (NFC) Tags:** With NFC-enabled devices, consumers can simply tap their smartphones against the packaging to unlock interactive content. This could include videos, loyalty programs, or augmented reality experiences that bring the product to life.

3. **Augmented Reality (AR):** AR experiences can be integrated into packaging to provide immersive interactions. For example, pointing a smartphone camera at the packaging could trigger a virtual tour of the product's origin or an interactive game related to the brand.

These technologies make the packaging an integral part of the consumer experience, enhancing engagement and fostering a deeper connection with the brand.

## Behavioural Insights

Understanding how consumers interact with connected packaging provides valuable insights into their behaviours and preferences. By analysing data collected from these interactions, brands can gain a clearer picture of what drives consumer engagement.

### Understanding Consumer Behaviour and Preferences

1. **Engagement Patterns:** By tracking which content is most frequently accessed or interacted with, brands can identify what aspects of their products resonate most with consumers. This can inform future marketing strategies and product development.
2. **Consumer Journey Mapping:** Analysing the paths consumers take through digital content can reveal how they make purchasing decisions. This includes understanding the sequence of interactions and the time spent on each type of content.
3. **Personalisation Opportunities:** Insights into individual consumer preferences allow brands to tailor content and offers to specific segments, increasing the relevance and effectiveness of their marketing efforts.

### Case Studies: Changing Brand Positioning Through Insights

A plant-based milk brand initially believed that their consumers were primarily lactose intolerant. However, by incorporating connected packaging and directly asking consumers if they were lactose intolerant, they discovered that 70% of their customers were purchasing the milk because they perceived it to be healthier, not due to lactose intolerance. This insight led to a complete repositioning of the brand's marketing strategy, shifting the focus from lactose intolerance to health benefits.

Similarly, a protein bar brand targeted mainly towards women discovered through connected packaging analytics that 20% of their consumers were male. This unexpected insight prompted them to adjust their marketing efforts to include men, broadening their target audience and potential market reach.

In another instance, a juice brand used connected packaging to survey their customers about preferred ingredients. The overwhelmingly positive feedback on a particular ingredient gave the innovation team the confidence to launch a new flavour, knowing it would likely be well-received.

These examples illustrate how connected packaging can reveal critical insights that challenge assumptions and guide more effective marketing and product development strategies.

**Advanced Consumer Insights from Scan Data**

1. **Popular Interaction Times:** By analysing scan data, brands can determine which days and times are most popular for consumer engagement. This can help optimise the timing of marketing campaigns and promotions to maximise impact.
2. **Social Media Influence:** Understanding how social media activity affects scanning behaviour is crucial. For instance, a leading juice brand discovered significant referrals and shares on Pinterest, prompting them to strengthen their presence on that platform to better connect with their audience.
3. **Demographic Insights:** Scan data can reveal correlations between specific SKUs and particular demographics. For example, a protein

bar brand learned that a significant portion of their consumers were men, leading to more inclusive marketing strategies.

4.  **Incentive Preferences:** When consumers choose which prizes they wish to enter for in a promotion, they provide valuable data on what drives and incentivizes them. This insight can inform future promotions and product offerings.

5.  **Prize Redemption Patterns:** Analysing which age groups are more likely to participate in certain prize redemptions can guide targeted marketing efforts and better understand consumer preferences. When allowing users to choose their prize there are fantastic insights as to what motivates certain consumer groups for example and then marketing strategies can be built around those learnings.

## Feedback and Analytics

Data is at the heart of connected packaging, providing a continuous feedback loop that can be leveraged to improve consumer engagement and overall brand performance.

## Leveraging Data to Improve Engagement

1.  **Real-Time Feedback:** Connected packaging enables brands to gather real-time feedback from consumers. Surveys, polls, and interactive features can capture immediate responses, allowing brands to quickly address any issues or capitalise on positive feedback.

2.  **Performance Metrics:** By analysing key metrics such as scan rates, engagement duration, and conversion rates, brands can assess the effectiveness of their connected packaging initiatives. This data-driven approach helps in refining strategies and optimising future campaigns.

3.  **Iterative Improvements:** Continuous data collection and analysis facilitate an iterative approach to improving connected packaging. Brands can experiment with different types of content, formats, and engagement strategies, using analytics to guide adjustments and enhancements.

4.  **GDPR Compliance:** Ensuring that data collection and usage comply with GDPR and other data protection regulations is essential. Brands must implement robust data governance practices to safeguard consumer information and build trust.

**Predicting Consumer Behaviour**

1.  **Behavioural Predictions:** By analysing past interactions and engagement data, brands can predict future consumer behaviour. This includes identifying trends in purchase patterns, preferences for certain types of content, and responses to various promotional strategies.

2.  **Scan Data Analysis:** Tracking scan data over time allows brands to understand peak engagement periods and correlate them with external factors like social media campaigns or seasonal trends. This predictive analysis helps in planning future marketing efforts more effectively.

3.  **Personalised Marketing:** Predictive analytics enables brands to personalise their marketing strategies. By understanding individual consumer preferences and behaviours, brands can tailor their messaging and offers to increase the likelihood of conversion and enhance the overall customer experience.

4.  **Innovative Insights:** For instance, a leading juice brand discovered a high rate of referrals and shares on Pinterest through connected packaging data. This insight led them to establish a stronger

presence on Pinterest, aligning their marketing efforts with consumer behaviour patterns.

By leveraging feedback, analytics, and predictive insights, brands can create a dynamic and responsive consumer experience that evolves based on real-world interactions and preferences. This not only enhances engagement but also strengthens brand loyalty and drives business growth.

# Chapter 6 - Designing and Implementing Connected Packaging

The art of creating effective Connected Packaging lies in striking a delicate balance between visual appeal and practical utility. This critical equilibrium ensures that packaging not only captivates consumers at first glance but also delivers a seamless and valuable interactive experience. At its core, successful Connected Packaging design is about reciprocity - carefully weighing what you ask of consumers against the experience you provide in return. The key is to create an enticing visual hook that draws consumers in, while simultaneously offering an intuitive and rewarding digital interaction that justifies their engagement. This balance extends beyond mere aesthetics and functionality; it encompasses the entire user journey, from initial attraction to sustained interaction and ultimately, brand loyalty. By thoughtfully harmonizing these elements, brands can create Connected Packaging that not only stands out on shelves but also fosters meaningful connections with consumers in the digital realm.

One thing that stands as a big difference between QRs and NFC is the fact the QR needs to be integrated into the artwork, brands are concerned with how digital triggers will affect the look of their packaging.

After almost 10 years of working with design teams on the design and implementation of QR codes and their digital experiences, I've tried to address in this chapter what I consider the key considerations for designers.

**Strategic Planning: Identifying Goals and Objectives**

Before delving into the design process, it is essential to outline clear goals and objectives. For Connected Packaging, these may include enhancing consumer engagement, improving accessibility, and ensuring traceability. A massive 96% of brands view connected experiences as pivotal in their marketing strategies. Therefore, your design should cater to these expectations while addressing any concerns related to the integration of digital triggers like QR codes and NFC tags.

Creating a connected experience involves a strategic approach that integrates business goals, technology, and design. Here's a step-by-step guide to strategically plan, identify goals and objectives, choose the right technology, and design the connected experience correctly:

**Define the Vision**

 - Establish a clear vision of what the connected experience aims to achieve. This could be improving customer engagement, tracking grey trade, giving consumer visibility on the supply chain, enhancing operational efficiency, or launching a loyalty program.

Think about  -

- Who is my target audience, and how will they likely use the QR code? What value am I bringing them?
-  What action or information do I want my target audience to take away from the QR code?
- Will QRs help us achieve our business and marketing goals?
- What data do I want to collect?
- How can I use that data?
- What is the value exchange between consumer and the brand - ie. Who wins what?
- How long will this be interesting content? When will I update the content?
- How will I track engagement?
- Does this content align with my target audience? Does it work if only access on mobile?

### Set SMART Goals

- **Specific:** Define clear and specific goals. If you are unsure about getting a consultancy to support you in this area it's better to start this correctly than learn along the way what options you need.

- **Measurable:** Ensure goals can be measured to track progress. Tracking is much easier in the digital world.. But what are you going to track? What will be the measure of success? Number of new customer records? Increase in sales? Engagement time? Reduction in fraud? Identification of fakes?

- **Achievable:** Set realistic goals. Seek advice on what might be the right success criteria if there is little known data.

- **Relevant:** Align goals with business objectives.

- **Time-bound:** Set a timeline for achieving these goals.

### Identify Key Objectives

- Break down the overall goals into specific, actionable objectives. For example, if the goal is to improve customer engagement, an objective could be to increase the consumer database by 30% within six months.

### Decide on Technology Options

Assess Requirements

- Determine the technological needs based on your goals and objectives. Consider functionality, scalability, integration capabilities, cost and user experience.

**Explore Technology Solutions**

- IoT Platforms: For connected devices.

- Mobile Apps: For customer engagement.

- Cloud Services: For data storage and processing.

- Data Analytics Tools: For insights and decision-making.

- AI and Machine Learning: For personalised experiences and automation.

**Evaluate Technology Providers**

When embarking on connected packaging initiatives, it's crucial to select the right partners. Look for vendors or agencies with:

1. Proven track records in connected packaging
2. A diverse portfolio of relevant case studies
3. Robust ongoing support systems
4. Compatibility with your existing technological infrastructure

While evaluating providers, compare their features, costs, and scalability options. It's important to note that while current digital and creative agencies can be valuable team members in connected packaging projects, they often lack the specialised expertise to independently manage these campaigns.

The field of connected packaging experts is relatively small but growing. Consider partnering with:

1. Specialised agencies like Appetite Creative
2. Consultants with specific connected packaging experience

3.  Industry organizations such as The Pack Hub or AIPIA (Active & Intelligent Packaging Industry Association)

These entities can provide the necessary expertise and support to ensure your connected packaging initiatives are successful and impactful.

**Prototype and Test**

Develop prototypes to test different technology solutions. Gather feedback from stakeholders and end-users to refine the technology stack.

**Designing the Connected Experience Correctly**

Ok let's pick up the crayons now...

**User-Centred Design**

 - Understand your target audience through research, personas, and user journey mapping. Ensure the design meets their needs and preferences. Remember also this will be on a mobile screen only so ensure this is designed for a small screen and responsive.

**Design Principles**

 - Simplicity: Keep the design intuitive and easy to use.

 - Consistency: Maintain a consistent user interface and experience across all touchpoints.

 - Accessibility: Ensure the design is accessible to all users, including those with disabilities.

- Responsiveness: Design for different devices and screen sizes.

**Feedback and Iteration**

- Even after launch, be constantly learning and updating the experience to ensure you are optimising the platform for the type of content and users you have.

**Design Considerations: Balancing Aesthetics and Functionality**

**1. Visual Appeal and Brand Consistency**

- **Visual Integration**: QR codes and other digital triggers should be seamlessly integrated into the design without detracting from the packaging's visual appeal. They should align with the overall brand aesthetics and not appear as an afterthought. It goes without saying that the digital experience, although allowing for so much more information and communication, must still be in line with the overall brand guidelines, colours, fonts etc. Having said all that, of course it is still important that the QR code is visible and is placed in a place which can be seen- NOT on the bottom of a carton for example.
- **Brand Elements**: Incorporate brand colours, fonts, and logos into the QR code design where possible to maintain brand consistency. This helps in creating a cohesive look that reinforces brand identity

## 2. User Experience and Accessibility

**Placement and Visibility**: Place QR codes and other triggers in easily accessible locations on the packaging. They should be visible and convenient for consumers to scan without disrupting the packaging's overall design. Consider the common usage scenarios and ensure the codes are placed where they can be scanned effortlessly. Remember the Quiet Zone refers to the empty space or margin surrounding all four sides of the QR code. This extra space helps the scanner quickly identify and recognise the QR code. We generally recommend 10-15% of the whole QR code dimension.

**Contrast:** A QR code should have good contrast between foreground and background colours, or else it will not be recognisable by the mobile phone camera. It's recommended that you use a light-coloured background (such as white, yellow or pink) with a darker colour for the foreground (such as brown, navy blue, and forest green). Do not be tempted to mess with it and invert it! Inverting the colours (dark to light and vice versa) of a QR code may look aesthetically pleasing, but it has a negative effect on its scanability. Doing so may change the pattern of the QR code and confuse the scanner, leading to an unsuccessful decoding process. Remember that the foreground colour of the QR code should always be darker than the background colour. Moreover, you should refrain from utilising shades of red, orange, and yellow colours in the foreground, as barcode scanners have a hard time recognising those colours.

**Readability and Usability**: Ensure that QR codes are of sufficient size and contrast with the background to be easily scanned by smartphones. Avoid placing them on curved surfaces or areas prone to damage, as this can affect their readability. We recommend 1.5x1.5 cm as a bare minimum. No matter how big a QR code is, if it's not sharp and clear enough, then it won't be read by a QR code scanner.  To ensure that the QR code is readable, make sure that all the squares of the QR code are crisp and clearly visible to the naked eye. Any attempts to stretch, shrink or skew the QR after it's generated could render it completely unreadable; so keep any modifications minimal. It's also really important that the printout is of high resolution. In general, for any size QR code, 300 dots per inch (DPI) resolution or higher is our recommendation for resolution.

**Personalisation:** Although standard QR codes are often dull and boring and will do nothing to capture the attention of passersby and potential customers, you also don't want to go too crazy with barcodes that are so beautiful that only a handful of phones can recognize them. With a little bit of creativity and personalisation, you can turn your QR codes into eye-catching visual elements that will stand out. You can add colours, graphics, and brand logos & images to your QR codes. You can also use branded fonts to make the QR code look more attractive and integrated with your overall branding strategy.

**Call To Action**-Ensure the Call to Action is prominently displayed on the packaging, encouraging consumers to scan. This captures your consumer's attention, but also somewhat reassures them, some people may be hesitant to scan a QR code if they don't know what's on the other side. Clearly communicate the benefits of scanning, such as "Scan to Win," which our research shows is particularly effective. Alternatively, consider "Scan to Play," "Scan to Find Out More," or "Scan for Prizes," "Scan for Discounts." It's crucial to convey to consumers why scanning will enhance their experience.

**Multi-Channel** -Using social media and POS massively increases the ability for people to be aware of the QR code and experience increasing engagement. The successful campaigns show the Call to Action promoted onpack, at retail, online and via their social channels and on other marketing channels.....And finally...

TEST IT!!!!

## 3. Functionality and Interactivity

- **Engaging Content**: Design the digital experience triggered by the QR code to be engaging and valuable. This could include behind-the-scenes content, interactive product guides, or exclusive offers. The goal is to enhance the consumer's connection with the brand and provide a richer user experience. Sending to a webpage or social media channel is not a good experience. This is not what I would classify as a Connected experience, this is just lazy.
- **Sustainability Considerations**: Utilise materials and design techniques that support sustainability. For example, Jabil's Connected Packaging solution uses recyclable materials and reduces the carbon footprint by minimising traditional packaging waste.

## 4. Security and Data Privacy

- **Secure Access:** Ensure that all digital experiences are secure and safeguard consumer data. This not only builds trust but also encourages more consumers to engage with connected features.
- **Transparency:** Provide clear and concise information on how consumer data will be used and ensure compliance with relevant data protection regulations. Transparency in data usage is crucial for building consumer trust.
- **GDPR Compliance:** Ensure GDPR compliance even when operating outside of Europe. Adhering to these standards ensures that consumer data is kept safe and secure.

**Implementation Strategies: Steps to Integrate Connected Packaging into Existing Processes**

- Implementing connected packaging into existing processes requires a strategic approach that aligns with both the technological capabilities and the branding goals of a company. At Appetite Creative, we developed a comprehensive methodology to ensure that the integration of smart technologies like QR codes is seamless, effective, and adds value to both the brand and the consumer.

  Below are the steps and best practices we follow to integrate connected packaging into existing workflows.

**Step 1: Define Objectives and Scope**

- The first step is to clearly define the objectives and scope of the connected packaging initiative. This involves understanding the specific goals of the project, such as increasing consumer engagement, providing product information, or driving sales through promotions. Stakeholders from marketing, design, and technology teams should collaborate to outline the desired outcomes and key performance indicators (KPIs).
- **Best Practice:** Conduct initial workshops with all relevant stakeholders to align on objectives and expectations. In my experience what might sound like a trade marketing initiative can also be a packing change, affecting the logistics team, finance team. If the strategy has not been set yet, set the strategy with a

consultant or team that can support you to understand the opportunities and implementations.

### Step 2: Assess Technological Requirements

- Once the objectives are set, the next step is to assess the technological requirements. This includes selecting the appropriate smart technology (e.g., QR codes, NFC tags), determining the digital content that will be linked to the packaging, and ensuring the necessary backend systems are in place. The technology chosen should be compatible with the packaging materials and printing processes.
- **Best Practice:** Leverage our expertise and case studies to ensure the chosen technology meets the project's needs and is scalable for future enhancements.

### Step 3: Design Integration

- Integrating the technology into the packaging design is a critical step. This involves creating visually appealing designs that incorporate QR codes or other smart elements in a way that complements the brand's aesthetic. The placement of QR codes should be strategic to ensure they are easily scannable without disrupting the overall design.
- **Best Practice:** Collaborate closely with design teams and packaging manufacturers to balance aesthetic appeal with functionality.

### Step 4: Develop and Test Digital Content

- The success of connected packaging largely depends on the quality and relevance of the digital content. Develop engaging and interactive content such as videos, games, product information, and promotions. It's crucial to conduct thorough testing to ensure the content is easily accessible and performs well across different devices and conditions.

- **Best Practice:** Conduct user testing to gather feedback and make necessary adjustments to the content and user experience.

### Step 5: Implement Quality Assurance

- Quality assurance (QA) is essential to ensure that the QR codes or other smart elements are functional and meet the project's standards. This involves testing the scanability of QR codes in various lighting conditions and on multiple devices, as well as ensuring that the digital content loads quickly, functions properly across all screen sizes and is recording all the data in the back end.
- **Best Practice:** Implement a rigorous QA process that includes both technical and usability testing. Basically, try to break it.

### Step 6: Launch and Monitor

- Once the connected packaging is ready, it's time to launch the initiative. Monitoring the performance post-launch is crucial to measure success and identify areas for improvement. Use analytics to track consumer interactions, scan rates, and engagement with digital content. The bet campaigns are also launched with complementary marketing.. With social, TV, digital all helping drive awareness.
- **Best Practice:** Set up dashboards and regular reports to monitor KPIs and gather insights for continuous improvement.

### Step 7: Maintain and Optimise

- Connected packaging is not a one-time implementation; it requires ongoing maintenance and optimisation. This includes updating digital content, addressing any technical issues, and iterating based on consumer feedback and performance data. Optimising in areas where people drop off and creating more of the content people most interact with.
- **Best Practice:** Offer maintenance packages that include regular updates, performance monitoring, and technical support to ensure the ongoing success of the connected packaging solution.

### Step 8: Scaling

- **Production Scaling**: Once the pilot is validated, scale up production while ensuring quality control. Collaborate with manufacturing partners to integrate new packaging designs into existing production lines.
- **Market Launch**: Plan a strategic launch of your Connected Packaging, leveraging marketing campaigns to highlight the new features and benefits. Monitor consumer feedback closely during the initial launch phase to make iterative improvements.
- **Data Analysis:** Analyse consumer interaction data to identify patterns and usage behaviours. Utilise these insights to refine marketing activities and ensure they are GDPR compliant. Continuously track and measure the performance of the connected packaging, integrating learnings to optimise future initiatives.

## Conclusion

Integrating connected packaging into existing processes involves a series of strategic steps that require collaboration, technological expertise, and a focus on quality. By following these steps, brands can create engaging and effective connected packaging solutions that enhance the consumer experience and drive business results. At Appetite Creative, we pride ourselves on our ability to seamlessly integrate these technologies into our clients' workflows, ensuring both innovation and impact.

# Chapter 7: Future Trends in Connected Packaging

## Emerging Technologies

This chapter delves into the exciting realm of emerging technologies that are set to revolutionise connected packaging. From artificial intelligence and machine learning, to voice activation, advanced IoT integration, and blockchain, these technologies are not just futuristic concepts but rapidly becoming reality in the packaging industry. They promise to enhance consumer experiences, optimize supply chains, and address pressing concerns such as sustainability and product authenticity.

Whether it's using AI for predictive analytics, implementing blockchain for authenticity verification, or creating immersive AR experiences, the future of connected packaging is brimming with possibilities that are limited only by our imagination.

As we explore these innovations, we'll uncover how they're poised to transform every aspect of packaging – from the moment a product leaves the factory floor to its interaction with the end consumer and beyond. These technologies are creating smarter, more interactive, and more sustainable packaging solutions that go far beyond the traditional role of containing and protecting products.

1. **AI and Machine Learning:**
   - AI will enhance data analysis from connected packaging, enabling predictive maintenance, supply chain optimisation, and personalised consumer experiences. Machine learning algorithms can adapt packaging

responses based on usage patterns, leading to more efficient and tailored interactions.

- o AI-driven analytics can predict when a product will need restocking or maintenance, ensuring seamless supply chain operations. There will also be much more intelligent uses in marketing and sales where predictive analysis and personalisation will allow personalised offers and ads sent to individuals based on their buying behaviour or predicted buying behaviour.

2. **Voice-Activated Packaging:**
   - o As an extension of AI and IoT integration, connected packaging is likely to incorporate voice activation technology. This will allow consumers to interact with products using voice commands, enabling hands-free access to product information, usage instructions, or even placing reorders.
   - o A consumer could ask a package of coffee, "How many servings are left?" and receive an audio response based on weight sensors in the packaging. Possibly it could even then be told to reorder automatically when only a week's portion of coffee is left.

3. **Advanced IoT Integration:**
   - o As 5G networks become more widespread, connected packaging will leverage faster and more reliable connectivity, enabling real-time tracking and monitoring of products throughout their lifecycle. This will also be

pushed by Extended Producer Responsibility legislation and other environmental compliances.
- IoT-enabled packaging can provide real-time updates on the location and condition of products, enhancing logistics and inventory management.

4. **5G Integration:**
- The widespread adoption of 5G networks will significantly enhance the capabilities of connected packaging worldwide. This next-generation wireless technology enables real-time product tracking, instant information updates, and more robust data transmission, further improving the consumer experience and supply chain efficiency.
- With 5G, packaging can stream high-quality video content or provide instantaneous customer service interactions through embedded communication devices.

5. **Blockchain for Authenticity:**
- Blockchain technology will likely be increasingly used to verify product authenticity and traceability, particularly for high-value goods and industries prone to counterfeiting.
- Blockchain can ensure the authenticity of luxury goods or pharmaceuticals by providing an immutable record of the product's journey from manufacturer to consumer. Especially where the rise in fakes is more than a problem I see a much wider adoption of this in luxury and pharma.

6. **Biodegradable Electronics:**
    - Research into biodegradable sensors and circuits could lead to more sustainable connected packaging solutions, addressing environmental concerns.
    - Biodegradable sensors can be integrated into packaging to provide connectivity while minimising environmental impact after disposal.

7. **Enhanced AR Experiences:**
    - Improvements in AR technology will allow for more immersive and interactive experiences, potentially replacing traditional product manuals or offering virtual try-ons for cosmetics and clothing.
    - Example: AR can transform a simple product scan into an engaging tutorial or a virtual trial, enhancing the consumer's interaction with the product.

## Market Predictions

This section explores key predictions and trends that are shaping the future of this dynamic industry. From rapid market growth to emerging technologies and changing consumer behaviours, these forecasts offer valuable insights into the evolving world of connected packaging. Factors such as sustainability concerns, personalisation demands, and technological advancements are driving innovation and adoption across various sectors. These predictions not only highlight the potential of connected packaging but also underscore its growing importance in brand strategy and consumer engagement.

Let's delve into the some market predictions that are set to define the future of connected packaging –

1. **Rapid Growth:**
   - The connected packaging market is expected to grow significantly, with some analysts predicting a compound annual growth rate (CAGR) of over 15% in the next five years.
   - Increasing consumer demand for interactive and informative product experiences is driving market growth.

2. **Increased Adoption in New Sectors:**
   - While currently prominent in food and beverage, pharmaceuticals, and cosmetics, connected packaging is likely to expand into other industries such as automotive parts and electronics.
   - Connected packaging can provide valuable data and interaction opportunities for electronics and automotive parts, enhancing customer service and product management.

3. **Shift Towards Sustainability:**
   - As environmental concerns grow, there will be a push towards more sustainable connected packaging solutions, including recyclable materials and energy-efficient sensors.
   - Brands will adopt eco-friendly materials and designs to meet consumer demand for sustainable packaging options.

4. **Personalization at Scale:**
   - Advanced printing technologies and data analytics will enable mass customisation of connected packaging,

allowing brands to create personalised experiences for individual consumers.

- o Personalised messages, offers, and product information can be dynamically generated for each consumer based on their preferences and behaviour.

5. **Smartphone Penetration and Adoption:**

- o The widespread adoption of smartphones globally has been a significant enabler for connected packaging. High smartphone penetration rates, especially in developing countries, have made it easier for consumers to interact with smart packaging solutions.
- o Brands can leverage smartphone capabilities to provide AR experiences, digital coupons, and real-time product information, enhancing consumer engagement.

6. **Always-On Communication Channels:**

- o Brands are moving from campaign-based communication to always-on communication channels. Connected packaging enables brands to maintain continuous engagement with consumers, providing updates, offers, and personalised content.
- o Instead of limited-time campaigns, brands can use connected packaging to keep consumers informed about new products, recalls, loyalty programs or special offers year-round.

7. **Trust and Adoption**

- o In the United States, 80% of users trust QR codes, highlighting their reliability and acceptance as a technology.
- o In China, QR code payments are particularly popular, with a vast majority of users preferring this method due to its convenience and security.

- This will continue to have a snowball effect to where customers will expect to see a QR code.

## Potential Challenges

While connected packaging offers numerous opportunities, it also presents significant challenges that must be addressed for widespread adoption and success. As we explore these potential hurdles, it becomes clear that the industry must navigate a complex landscape of technological, ethical, and regulatory issues to fully realise the potential of connected packaging.

1. **Data Privacy and Security:**
   - As connected packaging collects more consumer data, ensuring privacy and protecting against data breaches will become increasingly critical.
   - Companies will need to implement robust data protection measures and comply with privacy regulations to maintain consumer trust.

2. **Standardisation:**
   - The lack of industry-wide standards for connected packaging technologies could hinder widespread adoption and interoperability.
   - Developing universal standards for connected packaging will facilitate integration and scalability across different platforms and markets.

3. **Cost Barriers:**
   - While prices for sensors and smart labels are decreasing, the cost of implementing connected packaging solutions may still be prohibitive for smaller brands or lower-margin products.

- o  Economies of scale and technological advancements will be necessary to make connected packaging affordable for all market segments.

4. **Consumer Acceptance:**
   - o  There may be resistance from consumers concerned about privacy or those who find the technology intrusive or unnecessary.
   - o  Educating consumers about the benefits of connected packaging and ensuring transparent data practices can help mitigate resistance.

5. **E-Waste:**
   - o  The proliferation of electronic components in packaging could contribute to the growing e-waste problem if not properly managed.
   - o  Example: Developing recyclable or biodegradable electronic components will be essential to address environmental concerns related to e-waste.

6. **Regulatory Hurdles:**
   - o  As connected packaging becomes more prevalent, new regulations may emerge regarding data collection, product safety, and disposal of electronic components.
   - o  Companies will need to stay informed about regulatory changes and adapt their practices to ensure compliance and sustainability.

Before I conclude this chapter on emerging technologies, market predictions, and potential challenges in connected packaging, I spoke with **Paul Jenkins from the** Packaging innovation consultancy **ThePackHub** and asked a few questions-

**What emerging technologies do you think will have the biggest impact on connected packaging?**

Emerging technologies are set to really push forward connected packaging, offering brands unprecedented ways to enhance consumer engagement and streamline operations. AI and machine learning, which simulate human intelligence, will continue to improve exponentially, creating huge opportunities for predictive analytics and personalised experiences. Smarter smartphones will facilitate more immersive interactions through advanced augmented reality and faster processing speeds, while improved retailer in-store technology will seamlessly integrate online and offline experiences.

Advances in RFID and NFC technologies will make them cheaper and more sustainable, enabling widespread adoption for things like consumer engagement, inventory tracking and product authentication. Voice activation technology will also become even more mainstream and will enhance consumer convenience by enabling hands-free interactions with packaging.

**How does connected packaging fit into the broader omnichannel marketing strategies of brands?**

Connected packaging fits seamlessly into broader omnichannel marketing strategies by providing interactive and immersive experiences for consumers, enhancing engagement across all touchpoints. Brands can leverage the data collected from connected packaging to personalise marketing efforts, tailoring messages and offers to individual preferences across various channels. By facilitating real-time interaction and feedback across channels, smart packaging ensures that brands can respond promptly to consumer needs, creating a cohesive and responsive marketing process.

**What advice would you give to companies looking to start their connected packaging journey?**

For companies looking to start their connected packaging journey, it's crucial to first identify your primary goals of adopting this technology. Whether the aim is to enhance consumer engagement, improve supply chain transparency, combat counterfeiting, or drive sales, having clear objectives will guide your strategy and implementation.

Additionally, briefing Appetite Creative on these specific challenges will really help align your efforts and ensure that everyone is working towards the same goals.

**How does ThePackHub help brands navigate the complexities of connected packaging implementation?**

The most effective way that ThePackHub helps with connected packaging needs is in terms of insight. We have a world leading Innovation Zone and Patent Zone membership platforms that can help brands really understand what their competitors are doing and what the opportunity is.

**What are some common misconceptions about connected packaging that you've encountered?**

Common misconceptions about connected packaging include the belief that it is too expensive; in reality, the long-term benefits often outweigh the initial investment. Another misconception is that connected packaging is only for high-tech and premium products, but it can be applied across a wide range of industries and product categories. Some also think that consumers won't use connected packaging; however, when designed with user experience in mind, consumers are eager to engage with it. Lastly, connected packaging is often dismissed as just a gimmick, but it is a valuable tool that is here to stay, offering substantial benefits for both brands and consumers.

**Conclusion:**

So to bring a final summary to this chapter on emerging technologies, market predictions, and potential challenges in connected packaging -

The landscape of connected packaging is evolving at a rapid pace, driven by technological advancements, changing consumer expectations, and the need for more sustainable and efficient supply chains. As we've explored in this chapter, emerging technologies like AI, IoT, blockchain, and augmented reality are set to revolutionise how brands interact with consumers and manage their products throughout their lifecycle.

Market predictions point towards significant growth and expansion of connected packaging across various industries. The increasing adoption of smartphones, coupled with consumers' growing comfort with digital interactions, provides a fertile ground for these innovations to flourish. We can expect to see more personalised, sustainable, and interactive packaging solutions in the coming years.

However, this exciting future is not without its challenges. Issues such as data privacy, standardisation, cost barriers, and environmental concerns need to be addressed proactively. The industry must work collaboratively to develop standards, ensure data security, and create sustainable solutions that minimise e-waste.

As we move forward, the huge rise in the success of connected packaging will depend on striking the right balance between innovation and responsibility. Brands that can harness these technologies while addressing consumer concerns and regulatory requirements will be well-positioned to lead in this new era of packaging.

The future of connected packaging is not just about adding digital features to physical products; it's about reimagining the entire product experience. From enhancing consumer engagement and building brand loyalty to optimising supply chains and promoting sustainability, connected packaging has the potential to transform multiple facets of business and consumer interaction.

As we conclude this chapter, it's clear that we stand at the threshold of a new paradigm in packaging. The challenges are significant, but so are the opportunities. By embracing these emerging technologies thoughtfully and responsibly, the packaging industry can create more value, foster deeper connections with consumers, and contribute to a more sustainable future.

The journey of connected packaging is just beginning, and its full potential is yet to be realised. As technology continues to evolve and new applications emerge, we can expect connected packaging to play an increasingly central role in shaping the future of product experiences and brand-consumer relationships.

# Chapter 8: Regulatory and Ethical Considerations

## Compliance and Standards

### Key Regulations and Industry Standards:

**GS1 Digital Link:** This standard allows product information to be linked to a unique code, providing a consistent and reliable way to access product data. It's essential to ensure that connected packaging solutions are compliant and interoperable across different systems and regions.

**Food Safety Regulations:** Smart packaging must comply with food safety standards, ensuring that all information related to ingredients, allergens, and nutrition is accurate and accessible to consumers.

### Extended Producer Responsibility and Sustainability

As the global climate crisis intensifies, legislation is increasingly focusing on waste management and packaging. This shift aims to encourage and inform consumers about recycling practices, carbon footprints, and the journey of products and their ingredients.

The concept of Extended Producer Responsibility (EPR) is gaining traction, placing a greater onus on manufacturers to manage the entire lifecycle of their products, including the post-consumer stage. This approach is designed to promote more sustainable production and consumption patterns.

In response to these legislative changes, we can expect to see a proliferation of schemes and projects aimed at helping consumers better understand and engage with sustainability information. These initiatives may include:

1. Clear labelling systems that simplify recycling instructions
2. QR codes or NFC tags linking to detailed product lifecycle information
3. Apps that gamify sustainable consumer behaviour
4. Blockchain-based systems for tracking product origins and environmental impact

Such programs will likely be driven by a combination of regulatory requirements and consumer demand for transparency. As awareness grows, consumers are increasingly seeking products that align with their environmental values.

Companies that proactively develop innovative ways to communicate their sustainability efforts and guide consumers towards more eco-friendly choices may gain a competitive advantage. This could lead to a new era of packaging design where information clarity and environmental responsibility are paramount.

The success of these initiatives will depend on their ability to present complex environmental data in an accessible, engaging manner that resonates with consumers and drives behaviour change. As legislation evolves, we can anticipate a growing synergy between regulatory compliance and consumer education in the realm of product sustainability.

## Privacy and Security

### Ensuring Consumer Data Protection:

- **Data Encryption:** Protecting data collected from connected packaging through robust encryption methods is crucial to prevent unauthorised access.

- **Regulatory Compliance:** Companies must comply with data protection regulations such as GDPR in Europe, ensuring that consumer data is collected, stored, and used in a lawful and transparent manner.
- **Consumer Consent:** Obtaining explicit consent from consumers for data collection and clearly communicating how their data will be used helps build trust and ensures compliance with privacy laws.

## Ethical Marketing Practices

Balancing Marketing Goals with Consumer Trust:

- **Transparency:** Providing clear and truthful information about the product and its use of consumer data helps build trust. Brands should be transparent about the benefits and limitations of their connected packaging solutions.
- **Value Addition:** Marketing practices should focus on adding value to the consumer experience rather than purely promotional content. Interactive experiences, educational content, and personalised offers can enhance consumer satisfaction.
- **Avoiding Manipulative Tactics:** Ethical marketing avoids manipulating consumer behaviour or exploiting data for aggressive sales tactics. Respecting consumer preferences and privacy is key to maintaining long-term trust and loyalty.

# Chapter 9: Conclusions

## The Impact of Connected Packaging

As we stand on the cusp of a new era in retail technology, the humble barcode is undergoing a transformation that promises to revolutionise how we shop, manage inventory, and interact with products. Fifty years after the first barcode was scanned at a till on June 26, 1974, we are witnessing what industry experts are calling the "second barcode revolution" - the rise of QR codes in retail.

Recapping the key points of this transformative technology:

1. **Enhanced Functionality**: QR codes, developed by GS1, offer a quantum leap in functionality while retaining the basic checkout capabilities of traditional barcodes. They unlock a world of possibilities for both consumers and retailers.

2. **Consumer Empowerment:** For shoppers, QR codes serve as a gateway to detailed product information. With a simple smartphone scan, consumers can access crucial details such as allergen advice, nutritional information, and even the product's journey through the supply chain. This transparency empowers consumers to make more informed purchasing decisions.

3. **Business Efficiency:** On the business side, QR codes present a powerful tool for inventory management and waste reduction. By enabling more precise tracking of products throughout the supply chain, retailers can optimise stock levels and minimise waste. Damage can be tracked, logistics and supply chain and black market activity can be pinpointed. At the point of sale, these codes can instantly provide cashiers with critical information, such as recall notices, ensuring a higher level of consumer safety.

4. **Industry-Wide Adoption:** Major players like Tesco, PepsiCo, Walmart, P&G, L'Oréal, and Amazon are already testing and implementing this technology. GS1's initiative involves tests in 48 countries, representing 88% of the world's GDP, with these early adopters paving the way for global implementation.

5. **Ambitious Timeline:** GS1 aims for a comprehensive industry-wide rollout by 2027, facilitated by the ubiquity of smartphones and increasing consumer demand for product information and transparency. Although there is no legal obligation for this change it seems apparent that if the major retailers make this change then the brands will be forced to do the same.

6. **Versatility:** Beyond traditional retail, QR codes show promise in other areas, such as digital deposit return schemes in the UK, highlighting their potential in supporting sustainability initiatives.

Looking to the future, it's clear that QR codes are set to play a pivotal role in shaping the retail landscape. As **Anne Godfrey, CEO of GS1 UK,** aptly put it: **"In today's hyper-connected world, barcodes need to start working harder."** The transition to QR codes represents not just an incremental improvement, but a transformative shift that could rival or even surpass the impact of the original barcode introduction half a century ago.

## Summary of thoughts and recommendations

As we conclude our exploration of connected packaging, we stand at the cusp of a transformative era in consumer engagement and retail technology. The second barcode revolution, driven by QR codes and other smart packaging technologies, promises to deliver enhanced consumer experiences, improved business efficiency, and a more connected, transparent retail ecosystem.

To fully harness this potential, I recommend the following actions:

1. **Embrace Innovation:** Retailers and manufacturers should proactively explore and adopt connected packaging technologies. Industry leaders like Tesco are already paving the way, demonstrating the immense potential of these solutions.

2. **Educate Consumers:** Launch comprehensive campaigns to help consumers understand the benefits of interacting with connected packaging. Emphasise the wealth of product information, sustainability data, and personalised experiences that become accessible through a simple scan.

3. **Invest in Infrastructure:** Prepare point-of-sale systems and backend infrastructure to seamlessly handle connected packaging interactions. Tesco's collaboration with GS1 serves as a prime example of the necessary groundwork for this technological shift.

4. **Prioritise Data Privacy:** As data flow increases with connected packaging systems, implementing robust data protection measures becomes crucial. Transparency about data usage will be key to maintaining consumer trust.

5. **Include Sustainability:** Leverage connected packaging to support and communicate sustainability initiatives. The UK's digital deposit return scheme pilots illustrate how this technology can drive eco-friendly practices.

6. **Foster Collaboration:** Support and actively participate in industry-wide initiatives, such as those led by GS1. This ensures standardisation and seamless integration across different systems, benefiting the entire retail ecosystem.

7. **Drive Continuous Innovation:** Encourage ongoing research and development in connected packaging. While QR codes are at the forefront today, they represent just the beginning of this technological revolution.

As we look to the future, the trajectory of connected packaging is undeniably on an upward trend. The "always-on" approach inherent in these technologies is revolutionising brand-consumer relationships, offering unprecedented opportunities for continuous engagement and loyalty-building.

We are witnessing a significant shift in strategy among industry giants. Companies like Coca-Cola and Anheuser-Busch InBev (AbInBev) are leading the charge, adopting connected packaging not just as a novelty, but as a core, always-on strategy. This marks a crucial evolution in the maturity of connected packaging within the corporate world.

The industry is rapidly moving beyond the stage of pilots and one-off campaigns. Instead, we're seeing a strategic integration of connected packaging into the broader marketing mix. Brands are recognizing that this technology isn't just a temporary gimmick, but a powerful, persistent channel for consumer interaction.

This maturation process is reshaping how brands approach their packaging:

**From Campaigns to Always-On**: Rather than using connected packaging for isolated promotions, brands are creating ongoing, dynamic content strategies that keep consumers engaged over time.

**Integration with Broader Marketing Strategies:** Connected packaging is being woven into omnichannel marketing approaches, creating seamless experiences across physical and digital touchpoints.

**Data-Driven Decision Making:** The constant stream of data from connected packaging interactions informs product development, supply chain optimisation, and personalised marketing efforts.

**Enhanced Customer Relationship Management:** The direct line to consumers offered by connected packaging is being leveraged for improved customer service, feedback collection, and loyalty program management.

As we look to the future of connected packaging, it's not just the packaging industry insiders who recognise its potential. Major players in the e-commerce and retail space are also taking note. Amazon, a company known for its forward-thinking approach to retail, has been exploring the possibilities of connected packaging through its Transparency program.

**Güneri Tugcu, Senior Partner Manager at Amazon Transparency,** eloquently captures the transformative power of this technology:

**"Packaging is the silent ambassador of a brand, whispering its story to the world. In the era of connected consumers, it transforms into a gateway, offering brands an incredible opportunity to engage, authenticate, inform, and create lasting connections through the dynamic realm of connected packaging."**

As we've explored throughout this book, connected packaging represents a transformative force in the world of product packaging, marketing, and consumer engagement. The technologies and strategies we've discussed offer unprecedented opportunities for brands to interact with consumers, streamline supply chains, and contribute to sustainability efforts. However, as we look to the future, it's crucial to address both the challenges and opportunities that lie ahead.

One of the most significant challenges, as highlighted by **Ali Azhar, Global Product Manager at Tetra Pak,** is motivating consumers to engage with connected packaging. As Azhar points out, **"We need to come up with more than the average 'scan this, win that' campaigns but something to really get people moving for collective wellbeing or true interaction with the customer so we can understand their behaviour and deliver value."**

This challenge presents an opportunity for innovation in how we approach consumer engagement. The future of connected packaging lies not just in flashy technology, but in creating meaningful interactions that provide real value to consumers while also benefiting broader societal goals.

Azar envisions a future where connected packaging could play a role in reducing waste, lowering carbon emissions, or supporting causes like ending world hunger or educational initiatives. However, he emphasises that "this will only happen through a collective and collaborative effort between all industry players."

This collaborative approach will be key to overcoming other challenges in the field, such as:

1. Standardisation of technologies and protocols

2. Ensuring data privacy and security

3. Managing the environmental impact of smart packaging components

4. Integrating connected packaging seamlessly into existing supply chains and retail environments

As we move forward, the opportunities in connected packaging are immense. We can anticipate:

1. More personalised and context-aware consumer experiences

2. Enhanced traceability and transparency in supply chains

3. Improved sustainability through better recycling and waste reduction

4. New avenues for brand storytelling and consumer education

5. Data-driven insights leading to more efficient operations and targeted marketing

The future of connected packaging is not just about adding digital features to physical products. It's about reimagining the entire product lifecycle and consumer journey. By addressing the challenges head-on and embracing the opportunities for innovation, the packaging industry can create more value, foster deeper connections with consumers, and contribute to a more sustainable and connected world.

As we conclude our exploration of packaging's future, **Tim Sykes, Brand Director of Packaging Europe,** offers a comprehensive vision that encapsulates many of the key themes we've discussed throughout this book-

"Packaging has always been a connective medium, facilitating the material and communicative connection between producer and consumer. Today, as almost every human system is transformed by digitisation, it's both inevitable and essential that those connective functions of packaging integrate into the digital sphere. In our ever more complex world packaging is confronted with myriad demands. It has to be resource efficient while passing through supply chains characterized by far greater variety and unpredictability than ever before. The packaging and the product it protects will be held to account more fiercely in relation to its origins, authenticity and impact. It has to communicate effectively with a consumer both in a store and after unboxing in their home. It will need to be recycled, composted or reused. (Before long, other options will not be accepted.)

The ongoing development of connected packaging will address all of these demands. The smart package can be tracked from manufacture through every step until the point of sale or delivery, providing not just transparency, but data which, combined with machine learning, can optimise efficiency of our logistics. Connected packaging can give the consumer access to vastly more information about the products they buy than it's possible to print on a label, and down to specific details about the contents of the individual package in their hands. It can tell the consumer's device what they need to do with the package when it's empty, in their particular municipality, or tell the sorting line at the mix waste recycling plant which fraction it belongs in. It can take you to an encyclopaedic text with footnotes or playfully augment reality. It can talk to *you* as an individual: it can *know* you.

We already possess the fundamental technologies of connected packaging, from the humble QR code to digital watermarking to NFC and RFID. While continuing innovation is vigorous and necessary (in particular in bringing down the cost and footprint of these connective technologies), it seems to me that the next wave of development leans even more on imagination and standardisation. Standardisation – because people adopt tech when it fits seamlessly into our lives and existing technologies; when it becomes a ubiquitous thing, used by most people and applied quite universally. I expect the laws of commercial gravity will drive harmonization of how connectivity is incorporated into packaging and how consumers are invited to interact with it.

Imagination – because we are only beginning to tap the possibilities of this new world. I can envisage a utopia in which every package is digitally readable, and every package is digitally read whenever and wherever information is needed: in the warehouse, on the shelf, at the checkout, on the doorstep, in the smart refrigerator, on the kitchen worktop, in the reverse vending machine, at the MRF. The possibilities go further, and here (due to the limits of my own imagination) the utopian picture becomes hazy. From the point of manufacture in a smart factory to the point of recycling or reuse, the connected package is not only a medium to communicate data, but generates valuable data itself. Connected packaging can be the medium for a series of dialogues between an enterprise and successive touchpoints and users throughout its lifecycle. The opportunities to connect, process, share and harness the information that derives from these points of contact are vast, and still to be imagined."

**Final Word**

As this strategy matures, I've witnessed firsthand how connected packaging is cementing its place as an indispensable component of the marketing mix. I've been at the forefront of this revolution since 2015. Our journey has been one of constant innovation, pushing the boundaries of what's possible in the realm of connected packaging.

When I started Appetite Creative, connected packaging was still in its infancy. Today, it's a powerful owned media channel, transforming every product into a potential point of engagement, every package into a data collection opportunity, and every consumer interaction into a chance for brand building. This evolution has been both exciting and challenging, requiring us to constantly adapt and innovate.

The brands we've partnered with, those who recognized and harnessed this potential early, are now leading in this new era of consumer engagement. I've seen sceptics become believers, and small experiments turn into company-wide strategies. As we move forward, I'm more convinced than ever that connected packaging will be seen not as an optional add-on, but as a critical strategy deserving of significant investment and focus in any comprehensive marketing plan.

Moreover, as adoption increases, we can expect the costs associated with implementing these technologies to decrease. Simultaneously, the value derived from connected packaging is surging as more consumers become accustomed to scanning and interacting with smart packaging features. This trend excites me because it means connected packaging is becoming more accessible to brands of all sizes.

The increasing recognition and use of QR codes and other connected packaging elements and partners is creating a network effect that we're uniquely positioned to observe and leverage at Appetite Creative. As more people scan and engage, the data gathered becomes richer, the experiences more refined, and the overall ecosystem more robust. This virtuous cycle is driving innovation and value creation across the entire retail industry, and it's thrilling to be at the heart of this transformation. Now just imagine how powerful AI can be with this data set?

Connected packaging is not just a trend; it's the future of how brands will interact with consumers, how products will communicate their stories, and how the retail industry will evolve in the digital age. It's a future that promises more informed consumers, more efficient supply chains, and more sustainable practices - all areas where we at Appetite Creative are passionate about making a difference.

As we conclude this exploration of connected packaging, it's clear that we stand at the threshold of a new era in packaging technology. The journey ahead will require creativity, collaboration, and a commitment to creating value for both consumers and society at large. The potential is vast, and the future of connected packaging is limited only by our imagination and our willingness to work together towards common goals.

As this technology continues to evolve and integrate into our daily lives, it will undoubtedly reshape the way we interact with products and redefine the shopping experience for generations to come. The future of packaging is connected, and it's time - right now - for all stakeholders in the retail industry to join this exciting journey.

Those who embrace this revolution early will be well-positioned to lead in the new era of retail. The connected packaging revolution is here, and it's transforming every touchpoint between brands and consumers. At Appetite Creative, we're ready to connect, innovate, and help you navigate this new landscape. Are you ready to join us on this exciting journey?

Are you ready to connect?

# Glossary of Terms and Acronyms for Connected Packaging

## A

- **2D Barcodes:** Two-dimensional barcodes that can store more information than traditional linear barcodes. Examples include QR codes and DataMatrix codes. These are widely used in connected packaging for product identification and providing links to digital content.
- **5G:** The fifth generation of cellular network technology, which can enhance the capabilities of connected packaging by providing faster data transfer and lower latency.
- **AI (Artificial Intelligence):** Technology enabling machines to perform tasks that typically require human intelligence, such as visual perception, speech recognition, decision-making, and language translation. In connected packaging, AI can be used for analysing consumer data and optimising supply chains.
- **AR (Augmented Reality):** An interactive experience where digital information is overlaid onto the real world, enhancing the physical environment. In connected packaging, AR can be used to provide interactive product demonstrations or additional information through smartphones.

## B

- **Big Data:** Large, complex datasets that can be analysed to reveal patterns and trends, especially relating to human behaviour and interactions. This is crucial for analysing consumer data collected through connected packaging.

- **Blockchain:** A decentralised digital ledger used to record transactions across many computers in a way that prevents subsequent alteration. In connected packaging, it can be used to track and verify the authenticity and provenance of products.

## C

- **Cloud Computing:** The delivery of computing services over the internet, which is often used to store and process data collected from connected packaging.
- **CPG (Consumer Packaged Goods):** Products that consumers use and replace frequently, such as food, beverages, toiletries, and other consumables. Connected packaging is often used in the CPG sector to engage consumers and provide additional product information.

## D

- **Digital Twin:** A virtual model of a physical product or system that is used to analyse and simulate real-world conditions. Connected packaging can use digital twins for monitoring the condition and location of products.
- **Digital Watermarking:** A technique used to embed imperceptible digital information into images or patterns on packaging, which can be scanned for authentication or to access additional content.

## E

- **EPC (Electronic Product Code):** A universal identifier that provides a unique identity for physical objects, which is commonly used in RFID systems.

# F

- **Firmware:** The permanent software programmed into the read-only memory of a device. In connected packaging, firmware might be used in smart labels or sensors to control functionality.

# G

- **GS1:** The global organisation that develops and maintains standards for business communication, including those used in connected packaging (e.g., barcodes, RFID).

# I

- **IIoT (Industrial Internet of Things):** A subset of IoT focused on manufacturing and industrial processes, which can be relevant for connected packaging in production and supply chain contexts.
- **IoT (Internet of Things):** The network of physical objects embedded with sensors, software, and other technologies to connect and exchange data with other devices and systems over the internet. Connected packaging often leverages IoT to provide real-time data and interaction.

# M

- **Machine Learning:** A subset of AI that involves the use of algorithms and statistical models to perform tasks without explicit instructions, relying on patterns and inference instead. In connected packaging, machine learning can help in predictive maintenance and demand forecasting.

## N

- **NFC (Near Field Communication):** A set of communication protocols that enable two electronic devices to communicate when they are within 4 cm of each other. NFC is used in connected packaging for quick and easy data exchange, such as accessing product information with a smartphone tap.

## P

- **Printed Electronics:** The use of printing methods to create electrical devices on various substrates, which can be used to create smart labels or sensors in packaging.

## Q

- **QR Code (Quick Response Code):** A type of matrix barcode that can store a significant amount of information and can be read quickly by a digital device, such as a smartphone. QR codes in connected packaging provide consumers with access to product information, promotions, and more.
- **Serialised QR Codes:** QR codes that contain unique identifiers for each individual product item, allowing for precise tracking and tracing through the supply chain. Serialised QR codes help in product authentication and inventory management.

## R

- **Real-Time Data:** Information that is delivered immediately after collection. Connected packaging uses real-time data to monitor the status of products, track their location, and provide timely information to consumers and manufacturers.

- **RFID (Radio Frequency Identification):** A technology that uses electromagnetic fields to automatically identify and track tags attached to objects. RFID tags in connected packaging can be used for inventory management and tracking.

## S

- **SCM (Supply Chain Management):** The management of the flow of goods and services, which is often enhanced by connected packaging technologies.
- **Sensor Integration:** The incorporation of various types of sensors (e.g., temperature, humidity, shock) into packaging to monitor product conditions.
- **Smart Packaging:** Packaging that uses embedded technology to extend functionality beyond the traditional use of containing and protecting products. This can include features like temperature sensors, freshness indicators, and interactive labels.
- **Sustainability:** Practices that seek to minimise the environmental impact of products and processes. Connected packaging can contribute to sustainability by providing consumers with information on recycling and encouraging responsible consumption.

## T

- **Track and Trace:** Systems used to follow the path of products through the supply chain, from production to final delivery. Connected packaging often incorporates track and trace capabilities to ensure product safety and authenticity.

## U

- **UPC (Universal Product Code):** A barcode used for tracking trade items in stores. Connected packaging may use UPCs alongside more advanced technologies like QR codes and RFID for enhanced product information and interaction.

## V

- **Variable Data Printing:** A form of digital printing where elements such as text, graphics, and images can be changed from one printed piece to the next, without stopping or slowing down the printing process. This is crucial for creating customised and serialised QR codes or other personalised packaging elements.

## W

- **WebAR:** Augmented Reality experiences that are accessible through a web browser without the need for a dedicated app. In connected packaging, WebAR allows consumers to interact with products directly through their mobile web browsers.

## Z

- **Zappar:** A leading augmented reality platform and creative studio that helps brands integrate AR into their connected packaging solutions, enabling interactive consumer experiences through mobile and web applications.

# Resources and Further Reading

For those interested in delving deeper into the world of connected packaging, the following resources offer valuable insights and detailed information on various aspects of this rapidly evolving field. These books, articles, and websites provide a comprehensive understanding of the technologies, trends, and applications driving innovation in packaging.

**Books:**

**1. "The Internet of Things: Key Applications and Protocols" by Olivier Hersent, David Boswarthick, and Omar Elloumi**

   *This book provides a thorough introduction to the Internet of Things (IoT), which is a foundational technology for connected packaging. It covers key applications and protocols essential for understanding IoT-enabled packaging solutions.

**2. "Packaging Design: Successful Product Branding from Concept to Shelf" by Marianne R. Klimchuk and Sandra A. Krasovec**

   A comprehensive guide to the principles of packaging design, this book includes discussions on how technology is transforming packaging, with insights into connected and smart packaging innovations.

**3. "Smart Packaging Technologies for Fast Moving Consumer Goods" by Joseph Kerry and Paul Butler**

**4. "Active and Intelligent Packaging" by Stephan Selke**

**5. "Innovations in Food Packaging" edited by Jung H. Han**

**6. "The Internet of Packaging" by Andrew Manly and Jeremy Plimmer**

**Articles and Academic Journals:**

**1. "The Future of Smart Packaging: A Review" - Journal of Packaging Technology and Research**

This article offers an in-depth review of the latest advancements in smart packaging, including connected packaging technologies. It provides a scientific perspective on current trends and future directions.

**2. "Augmented Reality in Packaging: Enhancing Consumer Experience" - Packaging Strategies Magazine**

*An exploration of how augmented reality (AR) is being integrated into packaging to create interactive consumer experiences. The article includes case studies and practical applications.

**3. "Packaging Technology and Science" journal**

**4. "Journal of Packaging Technology and Research"**

**5. "Food Packaging and Shelf Life" journal**

**Websites and Online Resources:**

**1. Packaging Digest (packagingdigest.com)**

A leading source of news, trends, and analysis in the packaging industry. Packaging Digest regularly features articles on connected packaging technologies and their applications.

**2. Appetite Creative YouTube channel**

A pioneer in Connected Packaging, The Talking Giraffe Podcast and YouTube series offers insights into everything connected packaging. It includes case studies, white papers, and industry reports. Appetite Creative also hosts the yearly Connected Packaging Summit 4 years strong and ongoing :)

**3. The Dieline (thedieline.com)**

A premier resource for packaging design, The Dieline showcases innovative packaging solutions from around the world, including those leveraging connected packaging technologies.

**4. GS1 (gs1.org)**

An organisation that develops and maintains global standards for business communication, GS1's website includes valuable resources on standards for QR codes, RFID, and other technologies used in connected packaging.

**5. PackWorld.com**

Offers news and insights on packaging innovations

**6. ActiveandIntelligentPackaging.com**

Website of the Active & Intelligent Packaging Industry Association

**7. Podcast - CoCo: Click.Consume.Connect.**

A Podcast all about connected consumers, connected packaging and digital transformation. Hosted by Güneri Tugcu, Amazon, Senior Partner Manager, Transparency and Stefan Hills, the CEO of Linked, a packaging design agency.

**Conferences and Events:**

1. **AIPIA World Congress** (Active & Intelligent Packaging Industry Association)

Frequency: Annual

Smart Packaging Summit in Chicago 8/9 September

AIPIA World Congress Amsterdam 18/19 November

2. **Pack Expo events-**

Pack Expo, organised by PMMI (The Association for Packaging and Processing Technologies), is a series of trade shows focusing on the packaging and processing industry.

**1. Pack Expo International**

- Location: Chicago, Illinois, USA

- Frequency: Biennial (every two years)

- Description: This is one of the largest packaging and processing trade shows in the world, attracting professionals from various sectors including food and beverage, pharmaceutical, cosmetic, and consumer goods. It features exhibits of the latest innovations in packaging machinery, materials, containers, and automation technologies. Attendees can participate in educational sessions, networking events, and view demonstrations of cutting-edge technologies.

**2.Pack Expo Las Vegas**

- Location: Las Vegas, Nevada, USA

- Frequency: Biennial (every two years, alternating with Pack Expo International)

- Description: Another major event in the Pack Expo portfolio, this show serves the same industries as its Chicago counterpart but takes place in the western United States. It features extensive exhibits, industry-specific pavilions, and educational programs. The event also offers a focus on sustainability, showcasing eco-friendly packaging solutions and technologies.

**3. EasyFairs -**

Frequency: Annual

London Packaging Week, United Kingdom, https://www.londonpackagingweek.com/

Paris Packaging Week, France, https://www.parispackagingweek.com/fr/

Packaging Premiére & PCD Milan, Italy, https://www.packagingpremiere.it/it/

Packaging Innovations & Empack, United Kingdom, https://www.packagingbirmingham.com/

Empack Madrid, Spain, https://www.empackmadrid.com/es/

Empack & Logistics & Automation Bilbao, Spain, https://www.empacklogisticsautomationbilbao.com/es/

**5. Smithers**

Smithers runs several events focused on sustainability in the packaging industry. One of their key events is the "**Sustainability in Packaging**" conference, which is held annually. This event brings together industry leaders, experts, and stakeholders to discuss the latest trends, challenges, and innovations in sustainable packaging. The conference features sessions on various topics such as commercialized successes in packaging sustainability, e-commerce innovations, material and technology advancements, regulatory updates. There is an event in Barcelona and in the Middle East along with a whole host of other events such as "**Digital Print in Packaging."**

**6. Interpack**

- Location:Düsseldorf, Germany

- Frequency: Triennial (every three years)

- Description: Interpack is one of the world's leading trade fairs for packaging and processing. It covers the entire supply chain, including machinery, materials, and services for packaging and processing. The event attracts exhibitors and visitors from a wide range of industries, including food and beverage, pharmaceuticals, cosmetics, and industrial goods. It features innovative technologies, sustainability solutions, and trends shaping the future of packaging.

**7. ProPak Asia**

- Location: Bangkok, Thailand

- Frequency: Annual

- Description: ProPak Asia is Asia's largest and most significant event for the processing and packaging industries. It serves a wide range of sectors, including food and beverage, pharmaceuticals, cosmetics, and consumer goods. The event features extensive exhibitions, conferences, and seminars focusing on industry trends, technological advancements, and sustainable practices. It also provides networking opportunities with industry leaders and professionals.

## 8. PACK EXPO East

- Location: Philadelphia, Pennsylvania, USA

- Frequency: Biennial (every two years)

- Description: This event brings the PACK EXPO experience to the East Coast of the United States, offering a regional focus. It provides access to cutting-edge technologies, innovative solutions, and educational sessions tailored to the packaging and processing industry. The event caters to professionals from various sectors, including food and beverage, pharmaceuticals, and consumer products.

## 9. FachPack

- Location: Nuremberg, Germany

- Frequency: Annual

- Description: FachPack is a prominent European trade fair for packaging, processing, and technology. It brings together exhibitors and visitors from various industries, including food and beverage, pharmaceuticals, and cosmetics. The event features a comprehensive range of packaging materials, machinery, and services, as well as a strong focus on sustainability and digitalization in packaging.

**10. The Global Connected Packaging Summit -**

Where innovation meets insight in the dynamic world of packaging technology. Online Global Connected Packaging Summit in the Summer hosted by Appetite Creative, this summit aims to showcase how the integration of technology in packaging can lead to a seamless connection between the digital and physical worlds.

**11. The Sustainable Packaging Summit** – organized by Packaging Europe, this is Europe's leading event focusing on packaging sustainability, exploring both high level demands and emerging technologies on the innovation horizon that offer solutions, including digitization, connected packaging and AI.

Details of the next edition can be found at www.packagingeurope.com

**Industry Publications and Magazines**

1. **Packaging Europe** - leading resource reporting on the strategic demands facing

packaging and the areas of innovation responding to them. www.packagingeurope.com

- Provides news, analysis, and insights on packaging innovations.

- Features interviews with industry leaders and reports on market trends.

2. **Packaging World**

- Offers industry news, case studies, and technical articles.

- Covers topics such as packaging machinery, materials, and sustainability.

### 3. Svet Balení,

Svet Balení,

Which translates to "World of Packaging" in English, is a Czech professional magazine and online platform focused on the packaging industry. It covers various aspects of the packaging industry, including new technologies, materials, design trends, and industry news.

Audience: The magazine caters to professionals in the packaging industry, including manufacturers, designers, marketers, and decision-makers in companies that use packaging.

Content: Svet Balení provides articles, interviews, case studies, and reports on packaging innovations, sustainability initiatives, market trends, and regulatory updates.

Region: While it's based in the Czech Republic, it covers both local and international packaging news and trends, making it a valuable resource for the Central European packaging industry.

Format: It's available both as a print magazine and an online platform, allowing for wide distribution of content.

Industry events: The platform often reports on and sometimes organizes packaging-related events and conferences. The largest being OBALKO-the largest annual packaging congress in the Czech and Slovak markets, organized by the ATOZ Group, which also publishes Svet Balení magazine. It serves as a vital platform for packaging professionals to network, share knowledge, and explore the latest industry trends through keynote speeches, panel discussions, exhibitions, and sometimes awards, making it a key event for those interested in the Central European packaging industry.

Language: The primary language of the publication is Czech, but also some content in English or cover international packaging trends.

For professionals in the packaging industry, especially those operating in or interested in the Central European market, Svet Balení serves as a key source of information and industry insights

**Other Packaging Titles**

Packaging Scotland

Packaging Strategies

Sustainable Packaging News

Packaging Insights

Packaging Gateway

Packaging MEA

PKN Packaging News

Packaging News

The Packaging Portal

Packaging South Asia

Packaging Suppliers Global

## Online Platforms and Communities

### 1. LinkedIn Groups

  - *Packaging Professionals Group*: A large community for networking and discussion.

  - *Sustainable Packaging Group*: Focuses on sustainability trends and innovations.

### 2. Packaging Digest

 - Offers news, articles, and resources on packaging trends and technologies.

 - Provides webinars and whitepapers on various packaging topics.

### 3. PackHub

  - A subscription-based service providing insights and innovations in packaging.

 - Features a searchable database of packaging innovations and trends.


## Research and Market Analysis

### 1. Euromonitor International

 - Provides market research reports and data on packaging trends and consumer behaviour.

**2. Smithers**

- Offers market reports, forecasts, and analysis on various segments of the packaging industry.

**3. Mintel**

- Provides insights and reports on packaging innovations and consumer preferences.

**Other Industry Reports and White Papers:**

1. Reports from packaging market research firms like Smithers Pira, Mintel, and Euromonitor

2. White papers from major packaging companies such as WestRock, Amcor, and Berry Global

3. Ellen MacArthur Foundation reports on circular economy in packaging

4. Sustainable Packaging Coalition publications

**Professional Organisations:**

1. Institute of Packaging Professionals (IoPP)

2. Packaging and Processing Women's Leadership Network (PPWL)

3. Packaging Europe

4. Active & Intelligent Packaging Industry Association (AIPIA)

**Connected Packaging Awards:**

**The Packaging Innovation Awards:** Previously sponsored by Dow, these awards often recognise technological advancements in packaging. They are in their 35th year.

**M&M Global Awards - Category- Best Use of Packaging as a Media Channel in association with Appetite Creative** M&M Global awards programme. https://www.festivalofmedia.com/mmg/

**Pentawards:** Founded in 2007, Pentawards is an annual packaging design competition and online hub for packaging designers. Participants include designers, freelancers, design agencies, communication & advertising agencies, brands, packaging manufacturers and students. There is a category dedicated to "Brand Identity and Connected Packaging."

**The Dieline Awards:** While primarily focused on packaging design, they often recognise innovative and technologically advanced packaging solutions.

**PAC Global Leadership Awards:** These awards often include categories for package innovation and new technologies.

**AIPIA (Active & Intelligent Packaging Industry Association) Congress:** While primarily a conference, they sometimes feature awards for smart packaging innovations.

**DuPont Awards for Packaging Innovation:** These awards often recognise technological advancements in packaging.

Made in the USA
Las Vegas, NV
08 September 2024

94962609R00134